ROMA

ROMA
Modern American Gypsies

Anne H. Sutherland

Emerita, University of California, Riverside

WAVELAND

PRESS, INC.

Long Grove, Illinois

For information about this book, contact:
    Waveland Press, Inc.
    4180 IL Route 83, Suite 101
    Long Grove, IL 60047-9580
    (847) 634-0081
    info@waveland.com
    www.waveland.com

To Charles Louis
for his love, support, and technical savvy—
I am eternally grateful

Contents

Preface   ix

1 Why Study the Gypsies?   **1**
Fieldwork   4
History of the Richmond *Kumpania*   5
Basic Cultural Practices and
    Terminology of Richmond Roma   9

2 Roma History and Culture   **13**
The Traveling Culture   14
One Example of the Traveling Experience   15
A Note about *Romanes*   16
Effects of the Soviet Union's Breakup on Romanies   16
Studying the Roma   18
Conclusion   20

3 American Romani Identities   **23**
Four Roma Groups in the United States   23
The *Vitsi*   25
Other Romani Groups in the US   26
The Internet   32
Conclusion   33

4   The American *Kris*   **35**
The *Kris Romani*   37
The *Kris* as It Once Was   39
The *Kris* Today   44

5   Roma Identities and American Identities   **47**
United States v. Nicholas   49
Social Anthropology: Examining Cultural
    Differences in Legal Systems   56

6   Marriage, Fortune-Telling, and Luck   **59**
Marriage   59
Fortune-Telling   62
Luck and Mystical Ideas   65
Conclusion   68

7   Health and Illness   **69**
Fortune and Health   70
Cleanliness and Uncleanliness   71
Causes of Illness   74
Health Status of Roma   75
Death   77
Conclusion   78

8   Crime and Punishment   **81**
The American Judicial System   82
Rise in Crime and Violence   86
The Yanko Case   87
Global Influences: Recent Roma Immigrants   90

9   Changing American Roma Culture   **97**
Religion and Fortune-Telling   97
Technology and Traditions   98
Visit with Wally Davis and His Church   99
"Nostalgia"   102
Conclusion   104

Preface

The impetus for this book was an invitation from Peter Wagner, Director of *Romano Dzaniben* in 2014, to come to Czechia for the launch of a Czech translation of my ethnography, *Gypsies: The Hidden Americans,* and to speak at several universities where the Roma are studied. I was enthusiastically received by professors and students who had read my book and were struggling to gain their own understanding of Romanies. At three different universities where I spoke, the most often asked question was, what are American Roma like now and how have they changed with 21st century globalization? They urged me to write an update of my original book.

I returned from this experience with a new awareness that such a book would be valuable not only to American students but also to European students, as Europe is where Romani Studies programs have been created to understand what is viewed as a "Gypsy problem." I had gathered voluminous material over the years, but I set out to analyze the changes more consciously. This book is a summary of the Roma as they were in 1970, combined with articles I wrote on specific topics, such as health and crime, and new research based on my contacts with various Roma in 2014, who seemed to be acutely aware of all the changes in their lifetime and among their children and grandchildren.

The book comprises 9 chapters that include the analysis from my initial fieldwork, combined with global Romanies; American Romani identities; the Romani legal system; marriage and fortune-telling; an increase in serious crimes; and newly established "Gypsy churches."

Chapter 1: Why Study the Gypsies?—is an account of my research and the history of the Richmond *Kumpania*, highlighting basic language terms and the practices of the Richmond Roma.

Chapter 2: Roma History and Culture—discusses the Roma as a traveling culture, the use of many languages and discourses, and the effect of the collapse of communist regimes after 1990 on Roma in Europe.

Chapter 3: American Romani Identities—reveals the various Romani identities in the United States and the role of the *vitsa* in identity discourses as well as Romani cultural strategies for staying together in the era of global mobility.

Chapter 4: The American Kris—gives details on the *kris Romani,* a legal system that operates parallel to the American legal process, how it functions, and how it has changed and why.

Chapter: 5 Roma Identities and American Identities—looks at the differences between the American idea of individual identity (one person, one unique identity) and Romani corporate identity *(vitsa),* particularly in the context of the use of social security numbers.

Chapter 6: Marriage, Fortune-Telling, and Luck—focuses on changes in Romani marriage practices, Romani beliefs about fortune-telling and reading minds, and the ubiquitous concepts of good luck and bad luck.

Chapter 7: Health and Illness—discusses American Roma beliefs about health and the causes of illnesses, traditional Balkan practices and the modern practice of using doctors and hospitals, the connection of luck to health, physical and moral purity, and food. The Roma in America are not healthy and are prone to specific health issues. Their approach to death is also different from that of American society.

Chapter 8: Crime and Punishment—deals with the difficult issue of crime from both negative and false stereotypes of Romanies as criminals to the prejudices among law enforcement officers, judges, and juries, making it difficult for Roma to get a fair trial. The influx of many immigrant Romanies to America is changing the landscape of crimes.

Chapter 9: Changing American Roma Culture—explores the conversion to evangelical religions, the establishment of new Gypsy churches, the embrace of new technologies by young, more educated Roma, and nostalgia for the past.

I welcome your feedback. Please feel free to email me: annes242@gmail.com.

Acknowledgments

I owe a special obligation to the many Roma who let me into their lives and provided all the information in my two books. I do not name them out of deference to their wish for privacy unless they allowed me to do so. Insights from scholars of Romani, such as Elena Marushiakova, Vesselin Popov, Ian

Hancock, Carol Silverman, Paloma Gay y Blasco, Judith Okley, Matt and Sheila Salo, and the many scholars, from whom I have learned so much at the Gypsy Lore Society meetings, have all contributed to this book.

I am grateful to Peter Wagner, Director of *Romano Džaniben* in Prague and Margita his gracious *Lovara* wife who welcomed me into their home. Also Jan Červenka and Helena Sadíková of Romani Studies at Charles University in Prague, Hana Synková and Lada Viková of Pardubice University, Jaroslav Šotola of Olomouc University, and Marta Miklušaková who translated my book into Czech. The Czech publication was financed by the Czech Ministry of Culture.

I also appreciate the stimulating students at University of California, Riverside, where I taught a seminar on *Roma Migrations and History*, and all the support and wisdom of Janet Tompkins who guided me through the Gypsy maze.

Chapter 1
Why Study the Gypsies?

Between 1968 and 1970, having finished my formal education for a D.Phil. at Oxford University, I moved from England to the Bay Area of California for a two-year period of fieldwork on Gypsies, or as they are called now, the Roma. I had been offered a fieldwork scholarship from UCLA to study a then not much known group of Indians called the Yanomamo in Venezuela. But I had just married my life partner, another Oxford graduate who was going to Stanford for his postdoctoral research in biochemistry. I chose my new husband over a scholarship. This turned out the be the best decision I ever made because instead of being killed or worse by the Yanomamo, I decided to study the Gypsies in California and left the Yanomamo to the anthropologist Napoleon Chagnon.

It was very hard to get started with the Gypsies. When I approached a fortune-telling place and introduced myself as an "anthropologist," the lady at the door lunged at me and scratched my face with her long fingernails. Not an auspicious beginning, but, having grown up in a family of nine in Austin, Texas, a town that was even then an island of liberalism in a sea of oil and gas people, with an eccentric, and maybe even a little bit crazy, family, I had what Texans call "grit." Determined to prevail, I spent my time reading everything I could find on the Gypsies until I could get a break.

The literature on Gypsies was huge, full of exotica and romantic notions of Gypsies as well as portrayals of them as hopeless criminals who may steal a chicken or pick pockets as they wander through Europe. I encountered hundreds of books and articles on the "Gypsy mystique." An author's chance encounter with a Gypsy would inspire romantic descriptions of the mysteriousness of the subject and the occult practices of a strange, but fascinating people. The literature was amazingly consistent in its descriptions—Gypsies

1

were wild people, unfettered by social convention, living more or less cheer-fully in poverty on the margins of the world's societies.

Some of the romantic writers wrote truly wonderful books. Walter Star-kie, an Irish scholar, author, musician, and member of a prominent Irish fam-ily, was one. When I went to California to do fieldwork, I visited him at his home in Los Angeles. By then he was old and infirm, suffering from emphy-sema exacerbated by the choking LA smog. He died not long after I met him. Starkie was a fount of knowledge, which he had written up in numerous books of adventures with the "raggle taggle" Gypsies in Spain and England in the 1930s (Starkie 1935). But we did not talk about his life's work. We talked about how much something solid needed to be written, something ethno-graphic that simply (not a simple task) described who the Roma were, how they made a living, what their religious practices were, why they were always viewed as the pariahs of Europe. He thought perhaps social anthropology was the most useful discipline, although he himself had chosen a different route, the route of folk tale, anecdote, and story. His knowledge and insights were splendid. When I left, he bequeathed to me his collection of books and Gypsy Lore Society journals on the Roma. I had been trained as a Latin Americanist at Oxford, but Starkie's generosity of spirit convinced me to write an ethnog-raphy of American Roma (Sutherland 1986 [1975]).

At this time very little notice had been paid to American Gypsies and the literature on them was sparse. I studied the Welsh grammar of *Romanes* (the Gypsies' language, of which there are many dialects), put together by John Sampson (Sampson 1968 [1926]), and Gjerdman and Ljungberg's *Language of the Swedish Coopersmith Gipsy Johan Dimitri Taikon* (Ljungberg and Gjerd-man 1963). I tried to learn the language through articles by Tilhagen in the *Journal of the Gypsy Lore Society* (Tillhagen 1947, 1949, 1950, 1952, 1953, 1956, 1958, 1959), even though I knew their dialect would be different. In the meantime, I searched for some way to engage with the Roma, something I could do for them so they would be willing to talk to me. My good fortune was to meet a social worker, Janet Tompkins, who had a "Gypsy caseload" with Contra Costa County Social Services in Richmond, California, and had heard of my interest in Gypsies. One day she called me to ask if I could come up to Richmond from Palo Alto as fast as possible because the police were harassing the Gypsy parents because their children were not in school.

"The children are running wild all over the streets of Richmond. We need to do something fast to get them in school," she told me. I jumped into my recently purchased $100 1957 two-door, baby blue, two-ton Buick "tank" and gunned it up to Richmond. Janet and I reasoned with the police, and I offered to start a school specifically for Gypsy children to solve the problem for both Janet and the police. They were only too glad to cooperate, and so we started the "Romany School of Richmond," located in a room donated by one of the dying churches in that very poor community. We put out an appeal for volunteer teachers from the University of California, Berkeley, down the bay and were inundated with starry-eyed students dying to meet romantic, exotic Gypsies. The school ran for four more years, after I had left to finish my dissertation. Its success can be attested to the fact that the police even gave a grant from their police officers association foundation to keep the school running, as it solved their problem, too.

I took the role of "principal" for the school. We made the three leaders of the community (or *kumpania*) of Romanies the "school board."

> "Tell me what you want me to teach the students," I asked them.
>
> They were emphatic. "Nothing about Gypsies! Teach them to read and write!"
>
> "What about math?" I asked
>
> "No, they already know that and never make a mistake in calculating anything about money. They never get cheated!"
>
> Also, "Boys sit on one side of the room and girls on the other! If anyone flirts, tell me about it and we will kick them out of school."

Those were my orders, and I carried them out faithfully except for the last one.

Actually, it went very smoothly. We had about 30 children at any one time, ranging from ages six through 18 in one room, and since they were all related and their parents were aunts and uncles to the other children, they did not dare misbehave because the whole *kumpania* would know about it by the end of the day. The volunteer teachers taught the reading and writing, and I spent the day handling attendance and other school-related matters out in the Romani community.

There was always one family that had temporarily fallen out with some others, and I would know this because the children of those families did not show up for school. So after school I went to the houses to inquire why they were not in school and heard all about the fight from one point of view and then, from the other family, another point of view. From my point of view, this was priceless information, and I developed the habit of cross-checking everything I was told with at least three people from different families in order to get close to some reliable version of the truth. It was a technique the Gypsies themselves used, so they were happy with it.

What I did not do was take notes or use a tape recorder when I was with them or in their houses. Dialog and conversation was their preferred way to communicate. The question–answer method was anathema to them, and after finding that when I asked a question, I always got an untruthful answer, I avoided all questions, preferring to steer the conversation to something that interested me as well as them. But I honed my brain to remember conversations as much as I could, and every day I climbed into the Buick "tank" to drive back to Palo Alto, describing everything that happened that day into a tape-recorder as I drove. When I got home, I typed it all up on one of the original IBM Selectrics with the revolving ball (before word processing). This system of collecting data—conversations and observations—worked very well, and the Gypsies even praised me for the accuracy of my knowledge; however, I never divulged my information to warring parties or the police.

Fieldwork

In the meantime, the Gypsies taught me skills I had never imagined existed. Their observation skills, for example, were sharp and finely nuanced. They could size up a public context quickly and triumph over it before I had time to figure out what was going on. They could talk their way out of difficult situations with articulate ease. I learned to be more sharp-witted, to be more alert and mindful in any environment, to be more cognizant and analytical, and to expand my use of language beyond mere communication, to include the art of persuasion.

At first, however, even a six-year-old child could outfox me. Once when the Contra Costa County social services tried to persuade the children to go to a dentist, the children, who had never had dental work done on them, came to me, wailing that it would hurt—that they were afraid of the shot to numb their mouths. I was moved by their fears and assured them it was not that bad. "What does it feel like?" one particularly charming little girl asked me. "It's nothing, nothing," I said, hugging her. "It's just a little prick in the mouth." They exploded, screaming with pleasure that they had lured the "teacher" into talking "dirty."

Slowly I learned to hold my own with six year olds, and gradually I worked on honing my wits to the point that I could compete with the best tricksters. It was a challenge that I had to live up to in order to gain their respect. In doing that, slowly I began to see how they had managed to survive the adverse conditions of a pariah group for so many hundreds of years.

The Roma are a largely unknown ethnic population in the United States. Lacking census data, most estimates suggest there are now more than 500,000 members of various Gypsy groups living in all regions of the United States. Not all Gypsies belong to the same group or speak the same dialect or language. The Roma are originally from India. They migrated through the Middle East and Europe over the past 800 years, and the first wave arrived in the United States primarily at the end of the 19th century. They speak *Romanes* as a first language and English as a second language. Older Roma are generally not literate, but younger members of the family usually have some schooling and can read important documents to older members.

Roma live in urban areas, usually on main streets, in the poorer parts of towns. They are not always recognizable as such, especially the men who wear American clothes; however, women, in particular older women, often wear long colorful skirts and low-cut sleeveless blouses. They often prefer to pass as another ethnic group and some claim to be American Indian, Mexican, or Romanian. They are accustomed to discrimination and stereotyping by those who either exoticize them as free spirits or denigrate them as contemptible thieves. Neither stereotype is accurate.

History of the Richmond *Kumpania*

When I arrived in 1968 the *kumpania* in Richmond was, unbeknownst to me, of quite recent origin. It formed soon after the 1965 Watts riots in Los Angeles when the Roma living there fled the city and began to travel up the state of California to the northern counties. Three brothers, George and Staley Costello and John Davis and their big families arrived in Richmond where there was cheap housing, but by the time they got there they were destitute. They had faced this kind of mobility their whole lives and were accustomed to poverty. Their grandfather Matteo Costello was born in Montenegro on April 25, 1881. His occupation as stated on his birth certificate was "horse dealer." He migrated to Brazil where he married Baraselva Vasel who had been born in Brazil. Their son, Nicholas Costello, also a horse dealer, traveled from Brazil to Cuba from where he entered United States in 1920 with his wife Dara Mitchell and their seven children. Dara Mitchell's father had also migrated to Brazil from Europe in the late 19th century. Nicholas and Dara traveled from Brazil to Cuba where the US delegation issued a passport for them and their entire family. Their three sons grew up traveling across the US pitching tents in fields where a farmer would allow it. They ended up in Los Angeles until fleeing the Watts riots.

George and Staley Costello and John Davis were in the habit of going to the welfare office to get emergency funds when they were desperate, and so on arriving in Richmond, they poured into the Richmond welfare intake office. Janet Tompkins happened to be on intake duty when they first visited. and, as per the law, she informed them that in addition to emergency money, they could apply for aid through a new program AFDC (Aid to Families with Dependent Children), which had very recently been created under President Lyndon Johnson's Great Society programs. The Roma were thrilled and immediately referred to the welfare office as the "world's fair" office. Shortly after, George Costello, the eldest brother, died in Richmond and even more Roma poured into Richmond for his funeral, and they all went to the "world's fair" office. George's widow Geiga promptly burned his mattress in the back yard to the consternation of the neighbors who had already been complaining about the Roma practice of sweeping all the garbage out the back door. The situation was so chaotic that Janet Tompkins was given the entire Roma caseload, and she began to sort out who all the families were, get them medical aid, and help find them housing. They decided to stay in Richmond, and Staley became the leader of the entire Roma community.

Staley and Janet worked together to get the community to stop shoplifting. They had found a place where they wanted to stay, and Staley and the other two leaders, John Davis and George Lee, made sure no one broke the law. Anyone who did had to leave town. The leaders all invited the police to their St Mary's *slava* (saint day), to the Thanksgiving *slava*, and to weddings and funerals. The police had a bad relationship with the African Americans in California, so the Roma became their showcase of good relations with an ethnic group.

One community problem Janet Tomkins could not solve was getting the children to go to school. Even Staley could not convince the families to send their children to school. That was when I arrived and said that I would start a school for the children. It was a confluence of many factors—the need of both the social worker and the police to solve the school problem, my willingness to take on the school as a full-time job, my desire to create a way to have daily contact with the Roma community, and the eagerness of Berkeley students to teach reading and writing to an "exotic" group. In addition this was a time the government was reaching out to the disadvantaged, regulations about schools were lax by comparison to today's standards, and the Richmond Roma community was organized under an astute leader.

Even in 1968 the Roma in California were starting to live in houses, albeit within households with a somewhat fluid membership. Households generally

Romani School of Richmond, children receiving diplomas.

accommodated large extended families. Dating back to the days when they all shared one camp or caravan, members of extended families would eat and sleep at each other's homes as if they were their own. The men worked in groups of relatives and friends. Their usual work involved soliciting body and fender repair jobs, buying and selling cars, or helping women with their fortune-telling businesses. The women (mothers, daughters, and daughters-in-law) often shared a storefront office or room at the front of a house, where they could tell fortunes. The Gypsies preferred to keep to themselves and to avoid contact with non-Gypsies except as clients.

After I wrote my dissertation, I rewrote it into a book, *Gypsies: The Hidden Americans* published by Tavistock Press in 1975, now published by Waveland Press (Sutherland 1986 [1975]). That book focused on the political, economic, and social organization of the Richmond *kumpania* and analyzed the rationales behind their cultural practices. It was an attempt to answer the question: What is it in Roma culture that makes them able to survive in spite of leaving India over hundreds of years previously, moving across the globe, always living within another nation through massive cultural changes from the middle ages to modern times? I used an analysis of their deep structures, backed up by copious data, to tackle this question. What I did not know at the time, and to my great surprise, was that it would become the seminal ethnography of American Gypsies to this day, one read by anyone studying Romanies in America or Europe.

Rattlesnake Pete, Wally's grandfather.

This (current) book, *Modern American Gypsies,* contains a synopsis of the original book's answers to that question, but it is primarily an update on what has happened to the Roma and the Richmond *kumpania* since 1975. It also includes additional material, developed after the initial fieldwork that is not in the original book. Any reader who wants to know more detail about the original description of the *kumpania* can refer to *Gypsies: The Hidden Americans* (Sutherland 1986 [1975]).

Now, 45 years later I received an email from one of the boys in the Gypsy school I had run, Wally Davis, grandson of John Davis, one of the founders of the Richmond *kumpania*, who was now himself a grandfather living in Sacramento with his family.

> Hi, Anne, this is Wally your old Gypsy friend. It's been a long time. How are you? A lot has happened. My mom Ruby died. My oldest brother Nick passed away. They all saw the pictures you emailed me. That was great, we cried. Those were the best times in Richmond. Do you have any pictures of my granddad, Rattlesnake Pete? Do you remember him? Wow, Anne those were the best times—when Roma would get along and care for each other. If someone was sick they came to the hospital till the guards would tell them to leave. When someone would die, the whole Roma that was in town would come to the family and would stay round the clock not to leave them (the deceased) alone. I'm so glad Anne that I was in that time. A lot has changed, and for the worse. They forgot where we came from—our ways, our life, what we stand for, when our people fought to not change our way of life. Our freedom.

This book is to show Wally that, yes, things change, but the Roma still thrive 45 years later.

Basic Cultural Practices and Terminology of Richmond Roma

The term *Romani* (plural *Romanies*) includes Gypsies and other groups who identify themselves as Gypsies. Romani is the term used by many scholar activists to avoid the term "Gypsy" that has a pejorative meaning in many countries, especially in Europe. In contrast American Romani refer to themselves in English as Gypsies without apparent negative connotations for them. Americans mainly see them as romantic beings, also a form of prejudice, and the police see them as a band of criminals.

Because the term Gypsy is highly pejorative in many countries, the term Romanies refers to all the many groups that are loosely considered Gypsies, who spread out from India having migrated through the Middle East and Balkans into Europe in the 1400s and then to the Americas in the 19th century.

Rom refers to a particular individual Romani man and *romni* to a Romani woman.

Gadjo refers to a man who is not a Romani and *gadji* to a non-Romani woman. There is no word for all men and women. Human beings are either Roma or *gadje*.

Romanes (or Romani in English) is the language, of which there are many dialects.

Roma in my usage in this book refers primarily to four different divisions (*Lovara, Kalderasha, Machwaya,* and *Churara*) of *Vlax*-speaking (dialects heavily influenced by the Romanian language) American Romanies. There are also non-*Vlax*-speaking Romanies in the United States such as the *Boyash* (Romanian-speaking Gypsies), *Romungro* (Hungarian-speaking Gypsies), English and Irish Gypsies (also called Travelers), and Romanichels. As described here, the Romanies in the United States use the term Gypsy to describe themselves in English; for the most part they do not use Roma or Romanies.

The *vitsa* is the large kin group similar to a Scottish clan that is traced through either the mother or father (also known as a cognatic descent group). The name of the *vitsa* determines an individual's identity to other Roma. There is a hierarchy of *vitsi* (pl.), with some claiming superiority over others based on adherence to purity practices and evidence of good luck (*devla baXt*—literally luck from God).

Marime is a condition of spiritual and moral impurity. In addition to spiritual impurity it can be used to indicate that a *rom* or *romni* has been rejected or *boleme* (blackballed) from the Roma community for some moral transgression. Both leaders and the *kris* (the Romani legal system) can declare a person *marime*.

The American *kumpania* is a group of Romanies living in the same area, town or neighborhood, that is, in a specific territory. Some territories are wide open and any Romani can come and try to make a living there. Other *kumpania*, including the Richmond *kumpania*, consisted of Romanies who are usually related by *vitsa* or through marriage and constitute a controlled territory under the authority of a *rom baro* (literally big man). The *rom baro* deals with all non-Romani authorities (police, hospitals, schools, journalists, welfare office) and helps the Roma in the *kumpania* to make a living without creating problems with the *gadje*. He also defends the territory against Roma passing through and committing crimes, who, if they do not leave, he immediately turns over to the police.

The working adults in the *kumpania* have specific jobs by which they make a living. The women are fortune-tellers and work from a front room of a house where their family lives. A woman's clients are all non-Romanies, that is *gadje*. She advises on numerous issues—love, money, future luck, illness, and other matters. Some sell love potions or put curses on an enemy of the client. The women mostly handle relations with the welfare office for their families. The men form groups of brothers and cousins and solicit body and fender work at houses where they see a dented car. Some tar roofs and driveways going from place to place. If they are still a traveling group they may go as a large family to tell fortunes in Hawaii for a season or to the fields in California to pick crops during harvest season. They almost never take a job in a shop, restaurant, or office where they must work for *gadje*.

The American Roma, but not all Romanies, have a parallel legal system called the *kris*. The *kris* consists of a group of respected *rom* who adjudicate a conflict between two families or *vitsi*. It is handled by a *krisitori* (a much respected *rom* for his honesty, good judgment, and ability to bring the *kris* to a consensus; he must not be a member of any of the parties in the conflict). A case only results in the formation of a *kris* if the parties in the conflict have failed to resolve the crisis on their own or in a *diwano* (an informal gathering of the interested parties).

Roma traditionally do not marry according to American law. The preferred marriage is arranged by the coparents-in-law *(Xanamik)* who have authority over the young bride *(bori)* and groom. *Bori* is also a kinship term for daughter-in-law or sister-in-law depending on who is speaking. A marriage payment *(daro*—literally gift) from the groom's family to the bride's family solidifies the marriage and is followed by a wedding in which the groom's family dances in a *kolo* (line holding hands) with the bride; at the end of the dance, they put a *diklo* (head scarf or veil) on the bride, indicating that she is married and belongs to their *vitsa* now. There is a feast in which the men of the *Xanamik* families eat together at a long table where the *bori* passes around a hollowed out loaf of bread and the men put money into it for the couple. A marriage is terminated if the bride returns to her own family at which point her family must return some of the *daro*. The dissolution of a marriage is a major source of conflict among the Roma, so disruptive and sometimes violent that it results in physical fights, leaving the matter to a *kris* to resolve, or even the American legal system.

The Richmond Roma had many rituals. They celebrated Saint's days *(slava)*, Christmas, Easter, and the American holiday, Thanksgiving. All of these consist of the preparation of special food for the whole *kumpania* and eating together with lively conversation, music, and dancing, often barbequing a whole pig (that they would purchase live and slaughter) on a spit in the backyard. They may invite what they consider to be influential non-Romanies (police, officials from social services, or schoolteachers) to promote good relations with them. They also observe up to four death rituals called *pomani* (*pomana*, sing.), which also entail feasts, after the death and funeral, at which the deceased is represented by a person standing in for him or her. The *mulo* (which they translate as ghost) of the deceased has a place set at the table and attends the *pomana*. If the *mulo* is sat-

Slava with Roma, 2008.

isfied that relatives have shown the proper respect at each *pomana,* then the *mulo* gradually fades away. If not, the *mulo* haunts the people who have wronged it in life; their only recourse being to travel far away to escape the revenge of the *mulo.*

1. Compare the meaning of the following word pairs: *rom*/*gadjo, vitsa*/ *kumpania,* and *Romanes*/Roma. Indicate what significance they have in American Romani culture.

2. What aspects of the Roma have contributed to their cultural survival?

3. What is the Gypsy mystique?

4. What did the Roma want the author to teach and not teach in the Romani school?

5. How did the author collect reliable data when direct questions did not lead truthful answers?

References

Ljungberg, O., and Gjerdman, E. (1963). *Language of The Swedish Coppersmith Gipsy Johan Dimitri Taikon.* Copenhagen: Ejnar Munskgaard.

Sampson, J. (1968 [1926]). *The Dialect of the Gypsies of Wales.* Oxford, UK: Oxford University Press. (Originally published, Oxford: Clarendon Press.)

Starkie, W. (1935). *Spanish Raggle-Taggle Adventures with a Fiddle in North Spain.* London: John Murray.

Sutherland, A. (1986 [1975]). *Gypsies: The Hidden Americans.* Long Grove, IL: Waveland Press. (Originally published, New York: Free Press.)

Tillhagen, C.-H. (1947). "A Swedish Gypsy Investigation." *Journal of the Gypsy Lore Society* 26(3-4): 89–115.

Tillhagen, C.-H. (1949). "Gypsy Clans in Sweden." *Journal of the Gypsy Lore Society* 28(1-2): 119–134.

Tillhagen, C.-H. (1950). "Gypsy Clans of Sweden." *Journal of the Gypsy Lore Society* 29(1-2): 23–39.

Tillhagen, C.-H. (1952). "Funeral and Death Customs of the Swedish Gypsies." *Journal of the Gypsy Lore Society* 31(1-2): 29–54.

Tillhagen, C.-H. (1953). "Betrothal and Wedding Customs Among the Swedish Gypsies." *Journal of the Gypsy Lore Society,*32(1–4): 13–30, 106–124.

Tillhagen, C.-H. (1956). "Diseases and Their Cure Among Swedish Kalderasha." *Journal of the Gypsy Lore Society* 35(1-2): 49–62.

Tillhagen, C.-H. (1958). "Conception of Justice Among the Swedish Gypsies." *Journal of the Gypsy Lore Society* 37(3-4): 82–96.

Tillhagen, C.-H. (1959). "Conception of Justice Among the Swedish Gypsies." *Journal of the Gypsy Lore Society* 38(1-4): 18–31, 127–134.

Chapter 2

Roma History and Culture

I do not think there is any other people or culture in the anthropological record who have had so many "untruths" written about them as have the Roma. The Roma are very challenging to study partly because they have always obscured the notion of truth about themselves to outsiders. Why is this so? Partly, the Roma are indisposed to let people know the "truth" about them as it has been one of their most effective survival mechanisms. A group that is generally despised by those who live around them keeps its boundaries by *not* disseminating full and accurate information. They understandably sense that both inaccurate and accurate information can be harmful to them. Historically, their experience has been that both truth and untruth are subject to misinterpretation and can lead to castigation, discrimination, incarceration, and death.

The Roma practice of dissimulation has made description of even the most mundane Roma activity a very tricky task. No one who works with the Roma can say with complete confidence that everything they have written is fully accurate. There are only ways of being more or less accurate. It has been argued that this is true of all social anthropology, but the Roma are perhaps the most extreme example of the anthropological recognition of the complexities of truth and ethnographic lies. I believe the way to deal with this issue is to heed Clifford and Marcus' (1986) argument that anthropologists must find ways of writing ethnographies that, within a particular history, reveal how these historically situated subjects negotiate and communicate their particular view of realities. It is also very important to understand how those realities are shaped by global processes and agents of power such as states and nations.

The Traveling Culture

Historically the Roma are a *traveling culture*. Even Roma groups who today do not travel much are part of, and come from, a traveling culture. James Clifford, in his book *Traveling Cultures* (1997), brought to our attention the anthropological bias of privileging relations of dwelling over relations of travel. The emphasis on *in situ* fieldwork in our discipline, the phenomenon of Malinowski's tent (Benthall 2000) placed as a panopticon in the center of the village, focused our gaze on natives as dwellers of "A" culture in "A" place. In classic ethnography the anthropologist is the traveler who has come to engage in intensive participant-observation of the natives who are inhabitants of the village/culture.

The Roma are people who cannot be understood as site bound and must be understood as always having been the product of local/global historical encounters. Their history is of having lived in many places and countries, never in their own country and never speaking just one language. Because they have spread all over the globe, they have always needed many languages in which to develop discourses with themselves, other Gypsies, and outsiders. Given their historical relations of travel, they have always experienced the

Persa and Rupish Costello, dancing.

"local" in different groupings and settings, and not one local place. They have adapted their cultural practices to many historical eras and nations more than any other people since the Mongols invaded Europe and Asia. They have never lived apart from the world outside their particular cultural practices, but rather as interlocutors of multiple cultural historical locations. Their personal individual life histories often move seamlessly through many national and cultural boundaries all in one lifetime.

One Example of the Traveling Experience

When I met a *Kalderasha* Rom, *Staley le Stevanosko* (American name Staley Costello), he was living in a house he owned in Richmond, California. In that context he appeared to be a settled property owner. His great-grandfather, Matteo Costello, married Staley's great-grandmother, Baraselva Vasel, who was living with her parents in Brazil. His great-grandparents then left Brazil and worked their way by land through South and Central America up to Mexico. Records in 1920 show their son, Nicholas, had traveled from Mexico to Cuba and applied to the Legation of the United States in Havana, Cuba, to immigrate to the United States. At this time Nicholas and his wife, Dara Mitchell, had five children, three of whom were sons. Their sons were in order of age George, Spiro, and Staley. Staley and his brothers grew up in Central America and Mexico, but when Nicholas was 40 years old, he obtained a US passport in Chicago, Illinois. The family traversed the United States over and over, working as coppersmiths, buying and trading mobile homes, Dara telling fortunes, until their family was large, and they were getting into their 50s when they settled in Southern California.

Staley spoke English, Spanish, and *Romanes*. He spent part of his life traveling the United States in a trailer, moving from town to town or stopping for a while in the countryside. But he also lived in cities, urban pockets where rent was low. His grown sons were traveling with their families during my fieldwork off and on—to Alaska to trade for gold, to Hawaii to tell fortunes to American sailors stationed there, or to New York and Texas to visit relatives, attend weddings, *slavi*, and *pomani*. They would come back to Richmond for some time and then be off again. As far as the Contra Costa County Social Services was concerned, the Roma families in Richmond spoke broken English, were unemployed, collected disability checks for "personality disorder" and illiteracy, and had fixed abodes with addresses where they could receive welfare checks. However, this perspective did not reflect how they lived their lives.

Staley's family was part of the original big migrations from Europe and Russia in the later 19th century to Canada, the United States, and the other parts of the Americas along with that main wave of immigration to the New World. At that time anyone was welcome, and the Romanies immigrated along with millions of others fleeing poverty and 19th century pogroms. Most Romanies in the United States came during this period, and those American Romanies today who have been in the US for several generations are primarily descendents of those 19th century immigrants. My 1975 ethnography is really a study of a particular combination of *Kalderasha, Machwaya,* and *Cunesti* Roma who immigrated to the United States from Russia and the Balkan states. At the time I made that study I was mostly unaware of all those Roma in the Old World, because little was written about them, especially in English.

A Note about *Romanes*

Romanes is a Sanskrit-based spoken language with many loan words from places the Roma passed through over centuries (Persia, Turkey, Balkans, Eastern Europe) on their migration from North India. Each group of Roma speaks a different dialect of Romani, some which are mutually intelligible and some which are not. The Roma speak an inflected Romani developed during their time in the Balkans, Russia, and Eastern Europe. Other Romanies such as the travelers from the British Isles and the Gitanos speak a kind of creolized Romani combined with English and Spanish respectively.

The Roma I encountered in Richmond used a set of diverging, contesting discourses that changed with each dialog. With me they spoke *Romanes,* English, and sometimes Spanish all of which I could understand. They wanted me to speak back to them in English but not *Romanes.* "That is our language" they told me "not yours." Communication was not a matter of mastering "their" language, it was a creative set of discursive practices, in which both they and I were engaged on a daily basis through one or more languages.

Effects of the Soviet Union's Breakup on Romanies

What has most changed our understanding of Romanies in general was the opening to the West of Eastern and Central Europe and the new Russian Federation in the early 1990s when the Soviet Union collapsed. Romanies in the former Soviet Union and Soviet bloc nations—Hungary, Poland, Romania, Moldova, the former Czechoslovakia (now Czechia and Slovakia), and Yugoslavia (now Serbia, Croatia, Montenegro, Bosnia and Herzegovina, Macedonia, and Slovenia), and Bulgaria—for the first time since the end of World War II could freely migrate within those countries or emigrate out of those areas, mostly to Western Europe. Under communism the state forced Roma to be employed, but many of them continued to live in ghettos composed mostly of Roma. These segregated Roma communities have only gotten worse in many of those countries.

The largest populations of Romanies in the world are concentrated in Eastern and Central Europe (Liégeois 1995). In Eastern Europe alone there are an estimated seven to eight and a half million Roma.

Romania - 1,800,000–2,500,000

Bulgaria - 700,000–800,000

Hungary - 550,000–600,000

Slovakia - 480,000–520,000

Czechia - 250,000–300,000

Serbia - 400,000–450,000

Moldova - 20,000–25,000

In some countries, such as Slovakia, Bulgaria, and Romania, Romani are a sizable percentage of the population, as much as 8 to 10 percent. Large numbers of Romanies lost their jobs and safety nets in the postcommunist transition. Before 1989 all Romanies were forced by the state to be employed, but after that, unemployment among Romanies, for example in Hungary, rose to as high as 98 percent. Romanies recall the communist time with nostalgia because they always had jobs, but afterward they descended into desperate poverty. Not surprisingly, many began to migrate out of southeastern and Central Europe to Western European countries where today they are viewed prejudicially and as a source of many problems. Violence against Romanies has escalated and prejudice runs very deep. Romanies, for the most part, occupy the bottom strata of the economic system and make a living mainly in the informal economy.

Romanies who had lived settled lives for centuries along with Romanies who had been settled for 50 years in villages in Eastern Europe were renomadicized by the economic situation and the hostility of their neighbors. During the civil war in Yugoslavia in the 1990s, skinhead groups began to beat up Romanies, and communities of Romanies had their houses burned or were pushed out of town. I personally witnessed gangs of skinheads attacking Romanies living in a high-rise in Budapest while the police stood by and watched it happen. And in Bulgaria I visited a Roma neighborhood in the suburbs of Sofia, the capital, with only a spigot for water in unpaved streets with open sewers. They had only one elementary school for Roma children, which hardly went past the fourth grade. When I asked the principal what a Roma child could do if he or she wanted to attend university, he replied that the Roma did not go to university. These were the tumultuous transition years from communist control to independent statehood from 1989–1992, but the prejudice, segregation, and discrimination continues to this day.

After the formation of the European Union (EU) many of those former communist countries applied to join the EU, and to do so they had to acknowledge and accept the EU declaration of human rights for all EU countries. The EU Western and Central European states had to accept Romani migrations. Human right violations increased, and these governmentalities and nongovernmental organizations (e.g., The Soros Foundation) began to finance research on the Roma. Today the Romanies have become a focal point of research and human rights organizations to develop policies that deal with education and public services (water, sewage, housing, electricity), and fund numerous studies on discrimination against them in work, housing, education, and public health.

When Czechoslovakia split into Czechia and Slovakia, Czechia initially denied the Roma citizenship to the new country even though most had lived in Czechoslovakia for hundreds of years. This action rendered them stateless. This was changed due to pressure from the EU and other countries. Czechia is still considered to be lacking in human rights for Roma, and the public media present a very negative view of the Roma. When Yugoslavia broke up during the 1990s war, many Romanies fled to Serbia, Germany, Italy, France, England, and the United States. Some of those who stayed behind were killed by Kosovo Albanians, Croats, and Serbs. Italy, Germany, France, and England have also become hostile places for Romanies, especially Romanian Romanies who have been deported back to Romania occasionally (Knight 2013).

Studying the Roma

Under the communist government in Bulgaria it was illegal to study the Roma. Nevertheless, for many years Elena Marushiakova and Vesselin Popov

(2007) researched Romani populations in secret though they could not publish their research. When it became legal to publish on the Roma, they emerged as the ethnologists with the most valuable information on the different groups of Romanies in the former Soviet bloc. Their approach was ethnological focusing on specific characteristics (e.g., how they make their living, what languages they speak, and whether they have a *kris* system). When free to do research openly and publish their findings, they sparked a renaissance of studies and a mapping of the many groups in Russia, the Balkans, the Czech Republic, Slovakia, and in many other countries and in the British Isles, and others have been studying the Travelers since the 1970s (Gmelch 1991 [1986]; Kenrick and Grattan 1973; Le Bas and Acton 2010; Okley 1983). And later in Hungary Michael Steward studied the *Lovara* (Steward 1997). We now have research on a mosaic of Romani groups with many different languages and cultural practices.

Today both the study of the Roma and the field of social anthropology are newly positioned. There are more and better ethnographic descriptions of the Roma, providing a clearer ethnographic witness to a way of living that is in our midst but beyond our experience. Social anthropology is also now more instructive of, and open to the study of, life as a negotiated reality situated within history. The Roma are no longer an oddity among cultures; the way we described cultures in the past, as a culture living in one place, is no longer considered adequate. Because of these changes in the social discipline and in Europe, the Roma have moved from the margins of social anthropology to the center.

The biggest challenge today is that the realities of the Roma are perhaps more desperate now than ever before in that some groups of Roma have less of a niche in postmodernity than they did in pre-1989 modernity. There are encouraging signs, however. The Roma now have organizations formed specifically to deal with human rights issues. Political activism has been growing, and this has been effective in calling attention to discrimination and prejudice. It is also encouraging that some individuals are moving into political positions within the wider society. For example in 2003 an Irish town in Galway has chosen the first mayor ever to come from the Traveler group (Gilmore 2003). Still, in Central and Eastern Europe, these are not good times for the Roma. They suffer the highest unemployment of any ethnic group, severe discrimination that many, if not most, of the Europeans who live beside the Roma feel is justified. They have the poorest health statistics and level of education of any group in the region.

These conditions must change. In order for that to happen, both the Roma and state and local authorities will have to address some of their ways of doing business with each other. I will leave to others more closely involved with the European situation to comment on the means and strategies of those changes.

Conclusion

Paloma Gay y Blasco, a scholar of the Kalo Romanies of Spain, describes the Roma diaspora thus: "for over five hundred years, the Roma Diaspora has been characterized by its extreme political and structural fragmentation, and by the weakness or even absence of any overarching Roma imagined community" (Gay y Blasco 2002: 173). She notes that for centuries Roma have created a deterritorialized and highly mobile landscape of people loosely identifiable as Roma, but with little historical memory of ancestors or other groups (Gay y Blasco 2001).

Politically the Roma have always been decentralized, living in extended family groups, sometimes with a family head as leader of a wider membership but more often without such broad leadership. There is no internal system to unite the Roma into any effective overall political organization despite the best efforts of Roma activists and state governments. For a long time they have ignored historical memory beyond more than four generations of kin as befitting a historically mobile existence with no written language (Gay y Blasco 2002: 173–174).

They have embedded practices and mechanisms that protect the integrity of small family groups while at the same time allowing for changes in practices when needed. Over time, the waning of or the radical changes to the language, *Romanes,* leads not to assimilation but to fission or fragmentation from the group they inhabited. A range of purity practices to keep themselves separated from the *gadje,* for example, may be strictly followed to stave off assimilation in the next generation or kept at a minimum depending on local circumstances and degree of mobility. If purity practices become looser, especially when a group begins to settle in one area, occupation and residence boundaries create new areas of separation from non-Roma. This is the case with the Gitanos of Spain who have relatively permanent residences (Gay y Blasco 1999). The more mobile the group, the more the purity/impurity *(marime)* practices seem to be accentuated; the less mobile, the more the tendency is to construct other kinds of boundaries between Roma and non-Roma.

Over time they have developed mechanisms of flexibility, adaptability, and ability to negotiate many different local economies, social structures, and historical eras. According to Judith Okley (2003: 153), Gypsies lives "involve daily and ubiquitous encounters with non-Gypsies and non-Gypsy representatives." Roma have a long tradition, she argues, of cultural innovation that produces what has lately been called hybridity, one that emerges from culture contact rather than being undermined or destroyed by contact.

In the next chapter, I will discuss American Romani identities and more about the different Romanies who are living in the United States. We will also look at the changes in the many groups, their naming system, the role of the *vitsa*, and changes in strategies for coping with life into the 21st century.

1. What are the anthropological consequences of approaching ethnography as a traveling culture instead of a sited culture?

2. What is the difference between discursive practices and a language?

3. Why do the Roma have so little "imagined community" or historical memory? Is this an advantage for them or a disadvantage?

4. What does it mean to say that Roma flexibility and hybridity emerge from contact with other cultures?

5. What were the consequences of the collapse of the Soviet Union and other communist countries for the Roma?

References

Benthall, J. (2000). "Narrative: Malinowski's Tent." *Anthropology Today* 15: 18–19.

Clifford, J. (1997). *Traveling Cultures.* New York: Routledge.

Clifford, J., and Marcus, George E. (1986). *Writing Culture: The Poetics and Politics of Ethnography.* Berkeley: University of California Press.

Gay y Blasco, P. (1999). *Gypsies in Madrid: Sex, Gender and the Performance of Identity.* Oxford, UK: Berg.

Gay y Blasco, P. (2001). "We Don't Know Our Descent. How the Gitanos of Jarana Manage the Past." *Journal of the Royal Anthropological Institute* 7: 631–647

Gay y Blasco, P. (2002). "Gypsy/Roma Diasporas. A Comparative Perspective." *Social Anthropology* 10(2): 173–188.

Gilmore, T. (2003). "First Traveller Mayor to Be Elected Tonight in Tuam." *The Irish Times.* Retrieved from http://www.irishtimes.com/news/first-traveller-mayor-to-be-elected-tonight-in-tuam-1.365207.

Gmelch, S. (1991). *Nan: Life of an Irish Traveling Woman.* Long Grove, IL: Waveland Press. (Originally published, New York: W. W. Norton, 1986.)

Kenrick, D., and Grattan, P. (1973). *The Destiny of Europe's Gypsies.* New York: Basic Books.

Knight, S. (2014). "Home Invasion: The Roma of Park Lane." *GQ.* Retrieved from http://www.gq-magazine.co.uk/article/romanian-immigrants-park-lane-investigation

Le Bas, D., and Acton, Thomas (2010). *All Change: Romani Studies Through Romani Eyes.* Hatfield, Hertfordshire, UK: University of Hertfordshire Press.

Marushiakova, E., and Popov, V. (2007). "The Gypsy Court in Eastern Europe." *Romani Studies* 17: 67–101.

Okley, J. (1983). *The Traveler Gypsies.* Cambridge, UK: Cambridge University Press.

Okley, J. (2003). "Deterritorialised and Spatially Unbound Cultures within Other Regimes." In *Gypsy World: The Silence of the Living and the Voices of the Dead,* edited by P. Williams, pp. 151–164. Chicago: University of Chicago Press.

Steward, M. (1997). *The Time of The Gypsies.* Boulder, CO: Westview Press.

Chapter 3

American Romani Identities

The American Roma traditionally have had little interest in historical memory of themselves and no larger sense of themselves as an imagined community. They, however, do have a strong sense of identity, an essentialized identity that is rooted in kinship, language, marriage, and group practices, as well as timeworn ways of constructing and reproducing negotiations with the outside world. Because they move so much from place to place, their identity has to be modified or reconstructed for each new encounter with other Roma, non-Roma Romanies, and *gadje*. Over hundreds of years of migration, in my opinion, Romanies or Roma have developed a degree of cultural flexibility surpassed by no other peoples. They have forever lived within a dominant culture and nation-state where they have to negotiate with many forms of governmentality, economic systems, and historical periods. Their ability to negotiate many languages, and different cultures and states, is crucial to how they make their living—by persuasion, fortune-telling and salesmanship—and to deal on a daily basis with new situations. In this chapter, I will explore the many changes American Roma have made since my fieldwork in the late 1960s.

Four Roma Groups in the United States

American Romanies, as in Europe, include many different groups with different histories and identities. In some countries Roma is the generic term for all Romanies. I prefer to use the term Roma for a particular set of Romanies who divide themselves into "nations" or "races" (*Kalderasha, Machwaya,*

23

Lovara, and *Churara*) and *vitsi* (which are extended cognatic families for generations over at least 100 years) and speak *Vlax Romanes.* In the United States the largest group of Romanies are the Roma. They are divided amongst themselves into the following "Nations" or tribes.

1. The *Kalderasha*—The majority of the *Kalderasha* migrated to the United States from Russia and Eastern and Western Europe in the 19th century along with other immigrants from those areas. Some also went to Canada and South America but in lesser numbers. Their name refers to their occupation at the time of kettlesmiths who used to go door to door looking for copper kettles and pots and pans to repair. In the 20th century the men turned to auto body repair and buying and selling cars, recreational vehicles, and houses. They were traditionally highly mobile, traveling in groups of five to 10 caravans or tents in the early 20th century (later mobile homes), camping in the countryside between cities where they got work. The women told fortunes and sold flowers or other items when they passed through towns. They speak the inflexed *Vlax Romanes* as a first language, as well as other languages picked up along the way of the migrations. The *Kalderash* are divided into numerous *vitsi,* of which several were represented in Richmond. How many *Kalderash vitsi* exist today would be very difficult to determine since they are spread over North and South America, Europe, Asia, and various other parts of the world.

2. The *Machwaya*—They are a smaller group than the *Kalderasha* and consider themselves to be superior to *Kalderasha* mainly because they follow the purity rules more strictly than most *Kalderasha.* They migrated from the Balkans (Wallachia) and parts of the former Yugoslavia, bringing many customs from those areas such as *sarme* (foods) and *slava* rituals. The women were the most active economically because of their fame as effective fortune-tellers, a skill passed down from mothers to daughters and daughters-in-law. The women are also known for their knowledge of medicines and homeopathic cures they brought with them from Europe. Some *Machwankas,* such as Barbara Miller in San Francisco, became powerful leaders of a territory. In Richmond the *Machwaya* did not subdivide themselves into *vitsi* as far as I could determine; however, I have heard of *Machwaya vitsi* elsewhere in America, and it may be that they simply fail to use this subdivision because the *Machwaya* as a whole are a small nation. Another factor in the disuse of the *vitsa* names may be because of the prestige of calling oneself *Machwaya*

3. The *Lovara*—Those in the United States today came primarily from Hungary. They migrated after World War II and in 1956 when the Hungarian Revolution resulted in an exodus from Hungary. They work primarily as musicians with considerable talent. Before World War II *Lovara* traveled throughout France, Belgium, Netherlands, and Germany, but they were mostly killed, decimated in the concentration camps during World War II. There are *Lovara* living on the East Coast, in Houston, and in Chicago, but I never met one in Richmond,

4. The *Churara*—These are represented by one *vitsa* in Richmond, the *Kuneshti*. When asked directly, informants were not certain that the *Kuneshti* were a *Churara vitsa,* and many said it must be *Kalderash.* In Richmond they were there because of marriage alliances with the *Kalderasha.*

The *Vitsi*

Each *vitsa* theoretically may include all the male and female descendants of a real or mythical ancestor, who also may be male or female. In practice the *vitsa* includes only those descendants who count themselves as members of that *vitsa.* In accordance with the cognatic principle of descent, any descendant of an ancestor has the right to belong to their *vitsa,* but actually, only certain people "join" a *vitsa,* and most people eventually belong exclusively to one. The *vitsa* therefore is not a predetermined unit of persons and involves an element of choice. Generally, a person chooses to identify with the father's *vitsa,* and this has led many gypsiologists to believe that the *vitsa* is a patrilineal descent group (Cotten 1955; Pickett 1966). However, it is misleading to think of the *vitsa* as patrilineally determined since the Roma state that a person may belong to either the father's or the mother's *vitsa,* and even when the choice is the father's *vitsa,* that may change in later life to identify with the *vitsa* of the mother. The very word *vitsa* also gives no indication of a patrilineal tendency. *Vitsa* is from the Rumanian *vitsi,* which means family or stock (Ljungberg and Gjerdman 1963).

The Rom translate the word *vitsa* as "generation," members of one's *vitsa* being called "the Roma generations." This does not refer to genealogical level but is being used in the sense of "descendants" to indicate persons who have "generated" from one source.

It is also very misleading to think of the *vitsa* as a group in the way a *kumpania* is a group. The *kumpania* is a "group" because they all live in a finite territory. The *vitsa* is primarily a unit of identification, an "identity." The persons of one *vitsa* may never come together or function as a group in any way. Some *vitsi* are small enough to be a functioning group and a real body of persons, but most *vitsi* operate as a group only on two occasions: First, at a *kris*, it is said that the "*vitsi* get together." This is not a literal statement, since each *vitsa* is merely represented by a man and wife. However, at an important trial involving *marime* or *bolime*, the whole *vitsa* may attend since the situation gravely affects the *vitsa*'s reputation. In this case the *vitsa* unites as a group. The second occasion when a *vitsa* may unite is at a *pomana*, especially the *pomana* of a much respected *vitsa* elder. *Vitsa* members share an obligation to honor each other by attending each other's *pomana*, and frequently almost the whole *vitsa* may be present. Part of the reason for this obligation may be that a *mulo* only plagues relatives and affines, and this includes members of a *vitsa*. However, even for an important *kris* or *pomana*, when a *vitsa* is very large, it is not possible for it to unite.

Each *vitsa* has a name that may be derived from a real or mythical ancestor (the descendants of Pupa will be called *Pupeshti*). A *vitsa* may also be named after an animal, object, or defining characteristic of the people in that *vitsa*. For example, *Saporeshti* comes from *sap* (snake), *Kashtare* from *kash* (wood, tree), and *Bokurishti* from *bok* (hunger, hence "hungry people"). Some names are supposedly given in jest such as the *Papineshti* who were so named because they were adept at stealing geese (*papin* means goose).

Vitsi are formed and fragmented quite frequently. Some grow to be very large and famous, for the more prestigious a *vitsa* becomes, there will be more descendants who will ally themselves with the *vitsa*. When a *vitsa* becomes too large, several large sections of families within the *vitsa* may split off and begin calling themselves by a new name. Other *vitsi* may contain merely one large *familia* (extended family) covering three or four generations. A small *vitsa* such as this will be forced to marry with other *vitsi*, and if they intermarry closely with one particular *vitsa*, they may eventually merge with them. The majority of *vitsi* are large enough to contain several large *familiyi*.

Other Romani Groups in the US

Travelers and *Romanichel* are the Romanies from parts of the British Isles, some of whom came over on English ships with the British who settled in the United States, but most came later. There are English *Romanichels* and Irish Travelers as well as Scots Travelers. *Romanichels* speak Para-Romani (Matras,

2010), a creolized language that includes many Romani words or words of Romani origin. Irish and Scottish Travelers do not speak *Romanes* at all.

Boyash or Romanian Roma also speak an altered kind of Romanian. They migrated from the principalities of Wallachia and Moldavia (this is today Romania) where they have lived for several hundred years and were enslaved (Marushiakova and Popov, 2009).

By far the majority of Romanies in the United States are *Kalderasha* and *Machwaya*. They all recognize each other as Roma, though most are ethnocentric (viewing others from the point of view of one's own group) and refer to the others, such as the *Romanichels* and *Boyash,* as "not real Roma." Questioning the authenticity of other groups reveals a sense of superiority toward other Roma. As they have no overarching identity as being part of a global Roma population, they often express prejudice toward other groups.

Roma identity is rooted in kinship, language, marriage, and group rules, as well as in age-old ways of constructing and reproducing leadership to deal with the outside world. It is always *problematic* (meaning contested in that it has to be *reconstructed* for each new encounter with other Roma and non-Roma). "Rules" about the boundaries (Barth, 1998 [1969]) of kinship, lan-

American Romanichels in Switzerland with Ian Hancock.

Xoraxane Roma dinner in New York City.

guage, marriage, purity, and impurity are constantly adapting to local contexts. If over time use of *Romanes* wanes or changes in one group, other rules rise to the forefront. Purity rules include a range of practices that may be more or less followed, watered down, or kept at a minimum depending on local circumstance and degree of mobility. If purity rules wane, especially when a group more or less settles in one area, occupation and residence boundaries often become more important. The more nomadic the group, the more the purity rules seem to be accentuated; the less nomadic, the more the tendency to construct boundaries by other means.

Reproduction of identity (in the next generation) is an important task of the local group, one that is always beset by strains and difficulties. There is still much to learn about how Roma identity in different localities is constructed. We do have some identity "sites" or places in the developmental cycle of an individual with which to begin such a study, such as the naming system, cultural strategies, mobilities, and the system of authority including the *kris*.

Naming System

American Romanies are an example of a group always living in the borderline spaces of a dominant regime where they must constantly negotiate meaning and culture in the face of that contact. Over time they have developed proven ways to deal with encounters with non-Roma and non-Roma governmentality (all forms of government such as national, state, or local). One way is to problemitize (look at critically) identity through naming practices. Roma in the United States customarily have several names, at the very least three. First, they have a Roma name, which consists of a first name and then the first name of their father (e.g. Toni Le Stevanosko or Toni, the son of Stevan) and the name of their *vitsa* to indicate their primary identity. Everyone in the *vitsa* and in other *vitsi* knows the Roma name.

Second, each person in the family has a nickname that close relatives and friends use. George Yanko is called Ricky by his family, but other family members may use other names, including insulting or "dirty" names. Nicknames indicate familiarity and a jocular closeness. They can have more than one nickname among different family members. Knowing a nickname indicates a certain level of intimacy with the family.

Third, they also have several "American names" used mainly by non-Roma or by Roma when speaking to a non-Roma. George Yanko, for example, uses one of his American names for each business he conducts and one for each time he has had contact with governmentality, such as social workers or police. This helps him know who is calling or speaking to him and in which context. Very often in the case of arrest and conviction, the identity of the person by his or her Romani name is never revealed or discovered by law enforcement. The person is then convicted using one of the "American names." There are a somewhat finite number of American names that are used by Roma all over the United States, one of which may be on their birth certificate. Law enforcement authorities use one of those names or John Doe. Only recently has DNA evidence been used to make identification of the Romani individual in the future.

Balshaldi Hungarian Roma, Bill Duna and son.

Cultural Strategies

Roma in America brought their own parallel legal system (that is parallel to the national government) called the *kris*. The *kris* is a gathering of respectable adults and leaders in the community to sort out disagreements over marriage issues (such as the return of the marriage payment in a case of divorce) and moral transgression of individuals. Although Roma may fight with each other, they, in the past, avoided crimes of violence and major crimes such as burglary and major frauds. This has now changed. Not only are there more violent crimes, but conviction and jail sentences are not as easily avoided as they were in the past. Today, they are confronting new forms of surveillance, increasing contact with social services, and more severe punishments, both in the United States and in the European Union. It is my view that the recent increase in violent crimes, the increasing number of convictions, and the harmful manipulation of American law by Roma individuals indicate a transition phase in which the Roma are facing new challenges in their ability to negotiate with the regimes of the state. At the same time the parallel legal system, the *kris*, is being weakened by challenges to its authority from within by both Romanies new to the United States and the younger generation. This weakening of the authority of the *kris* on moral and economic issues and the fact that the *kris* does not deal with violence and murder are creating havoc with Romanies' ability to adapt to the changing nature of the American state.

There are various ways the American Roma are struggling to come to terms with these new challenges and reassert the authority of the *kris*. In their view, strengthening the authority of the *Xanamik* and the marriage bond is key to their renewal of the *kris*. In the meantime they are facing a grim future of increasing incarceration and state-sanctioned death penalty.

If the concept of culture is being replaced by a narrative of an imaginatively constructed context of knowledge systems, as George Marcus asserts (Marcus 1995, 1998; Marcus and Fischer 1999), then what we are looking at here is an American legal knowledge system overlapping with a Roma legal knowledge system in which each system has only partial knowledge of the other. Both the Roma and the officers of American courts are defined by what they know as well as what they don't know. What they don't know about each other often ends in producing injustice.

Mobilities

Everyone, including the Roma, is experiencing increased mobility globally and the consequent use of new technologies of surveillance due to the US

Patriot Act. How does this change the position of Roma relative to the state and other forms of governmentality? Are the mechanisms they developed over centuries working well in the 21st century?

To answer these questions, I will address recent development among American Roma in the types of crimes they engage in, the increase in violence between American Roma groups, and the level of sophistication and education needed for large-scale frauds by Roma. It has also been noted by a number of scholars that among the Roma alcoholism, violence, and drug use have become ubiquitous. In the 45 years that I have been studying the Roma in the United States, I know of less than a handful of murder charges and convictions. It is possible that this is due to the extreme mobility of the Roma for cultural and economic reasons, which meant that they were rarely caught or convicted. Some reasons include religious ceremonies (e.g., St. Mary's *slava*, Thanksgiving, Christmas), marriage and funerals (there are four *pomani* after a person dies), and other family gatherings, as well as the ability to work in different parts of the country where prospects for fortune-telling or other jobs are more fruitful. In the past, Roma were able to leave an area where they were in danger of being accused of a crime (rightly or wrongly). Their behavior has always been viewed as suspicious. For example, they often fled accusations of kidnapping children from towns that they passed through. I know of no case in the literature in which Roma actually kidnapped children, although they often were the scapegoats when children in a community went missing.

Moving by Roma is no longer effective as a means of avoiding *gadje* authorities. There are now very sophisticated systems for identifying, tracking, and finding individuals across the United States. These include computerized systems of vehicle registration, fingerprints, DNA, and forms of identification (Social Security numbers, driver's licenses, bank accounts, credit cards). Because of this increased and increasingly sophisticated intrusive surveillance, the Roma are being apprehended more frequently, convicted, and imprisoned. Today, they are aware that moving to another town or state does not protect them anymore, but they have not yet adapted to these new surveillance mechanisms and laws. (Specific cases of Roma crimes are discussed in chapter 8.)

Authority

The Roma have had a strong authority structure with the eldest family members being the leaders of their families and *vitsa*. In the *kumpania*, the one who becomes the "head" of a territory is the one who can negotiate best with the *gadje* community and cross over the lines of the local *vitsi*. Leaders emerge by means of their family ties, strong personalities, and the respect for their wives. The leader who prevails influences the boundaries of *vitsa* identity and determines to some extent who is included and who is excluded from living in the *kumpania*.

Young family members are expected to respect their elders and consult them about all major decisions as well as give the elders their earnings to distribute to other members of the *vitsa*. When a leader dies, the *kumpania* goes through a traumatic period of transition and may split up or regroup under another leader. This has always been a point of tension, and some *vitsi* do not survive it without fragmentation and weakening of the *vitsa*. However, new formations of groups of relatives try to find an elder to be the organizer and problem solver of the group. *Vitsi* that succeed at the succession of authority become wealthier and more stable. Today, the authority structure in the United States and in Sweden is weakened but by no means gone. The weakening is also linked to the rise in crime, drugs, and violence.

George Yanko, as an example, was raised by his grandparents (the most powerful elders of his family). He grew up surrounded by aunts and uncles and all his cousins within a strong authority structure. When his grandparents and soon after his father died, he and his brothers were without leadership as a *vitsa* and family. When this happens the family loses status and influence with other Roma. Their standing in the *kumpania* suffers, and the individuals in the family lose a great deal of the economic and social support system. One older brother has taken a kind of leadership role, but it is not strong enough to hold the family together, and the family seems to have stayed fragmented.

George is one of the older brothers, and because he was favored by his grandparents and raised by them, he was supposed to step into the "chair," but he did not due to his drug use, criminal record, and possible mental illness. His mother also was not able to assume the leadership role due to her mental illness. Today, the different families of the *vitsa* are scattered across the East Coast of the United States. Individuals in those families are opting not to marry another Roma or follow the general Roma custom and life styles.

The Internet

There has been growing contact between Roma of different groups and ways particularly for young people to communicate with other Roma. Whereas in the past, information and gossip was disseminated by word of mouth, now there are many ways to communicate outside one's family. In Los Angeles, for example, there is a "Gypsy hotline" where callers can leave messages about happenings all over the enormous LA area. New Roma arrivals to the United States post messages and videos on YouTube, Facebook, Twitter, and through email. They can show weddings to relatives left behind in their migration, meet up on Facebook in search of a Roma mate of one's own choosing, and in general increase the range of contacts they have with other Roma.

For example, a mostly unstudied area of Roma life is when an individual wants to veer from the group and leave the immense social pressure that life as a *rom* or *romni* entails. This venue is opening up because of the Internet. Through the Internet, I have now met a number of Roma who have left the fold. They found me by doing a search for Roma on the web and reading my book. I am in touch with a *rom* videographer in Sacramento, a *romni* housewife in North Carolina, and other *rom* and *romni* who no longer live within the Roma community. Earlier in my fieldwork I had no way to contact them because they were outcast from the Roma community or chose to leave. These Roma have a particular take on the community itself. Very often it is the recent conversion to evangelical Christianity that underlies their exit from their traditions. One *Machwaya* woman on video spoke eloquently of being liberated from the authority of her father and father-in-law because she now answers to a higher authority, Jesus Christ.

Conclusion

Roma survival strategies are being tested in many countries by globalization. American Roma have in the past been very mobile. They moved to find new economic niches or to avoid a conflict with American law or with other Romanies. Their practice of using many non-Roma names and keeping their Roma identities secret has facilitated their mobility as a way to solve problems. But these practices are no longer effective in an age of more effective surveillance techniques such as cameras in stores, and on streets and highways, as well as DNA evidence to identify an individual no matter what name he or she uses. Now the wider society and law enforcement personnel are more aware of Romanies, though not necessarily well informed about them. There are a number of police detectives or former detectives who consider themselves to be experts on a special category of what they call "Gypsy crimes." They have been very prejudicial in pursuing so-called Gypsy crimes and tend to believe that most Roma are criminals.

In the next chapter I will explain more about the Roma *kris* and other forms of social control. All of the authority structures, social control mechanisms, and organized *kumpania* are showing signs of enormous changes since the 45 years of my initial research (Sutherland 1986 [1975]).

1. If Roma identities are not based on historical memory like other cultures does that help the Roma?
2. What are the main "nations" of the *Vlax*-speaking Roma in the United States?
3. What does it mean to be ethnocentric? Is this common in most or all cultures? Give an example of ethnocentricity from your culture.
4. How do the naming system, mobilities, and changes in the *kris* and authority structure affect Roma contact with the American legal system?
5. How has the Internet and social media affected the American Roma?

References

Barth, F. (1998). *Ethnic Groups and Boundaries: The Social Organization of Culture Difference.* Long Grove, IL: Waveland Press. (Originally published, Oslo: Scandinavian University Press, 1969.)

Cotten, R. (1955). "An Anthropologist Looks at Gypsology." *Journal of the Gypsy Lore Society* 34(1-2): 20–36.

Ljungberg, O., Gjerdman, Edward, and Taikon, J. D. (1963). *Language of the Swedish Coppersmith Gipsy.* Copenhagen: Ejnar Munskgaard.

Marcus, G. E. (1995). "Ethnography in/of the World System: The Emergence of Multi-sited Ethnography." *Annual Review of Anthropology* 24: 95–117.

Marcus, G. E. (1998). *Ethnography Through Thick and Thin.* Princeton, NJ: Princeton University Press.

Marcus, G. E., and Fischer, Michael M. J. (1999). *Anthropology as Cultural Critique: An Experimental Moment in the Human Sciences.* London: University of Chicago Press Ltd.

Marushiakova, Elena, and Popov, Vesselin (2009). "Gypsy Slavery in Wallachia and Moldavia." In *Nationalisms Today,* edited by T. Kamusell and K. Jaskulowski, pp. 89–124. Oxford: Peter Lang.

Matras, Y. (2010). *Romani in Britain. The Afterlife of a Language.* Edinburgh, Scotland: Edinburgh University Press.

Pickett, D. W. (1966). "The Gypsies of Mexico." *Journal of the Gypsy Lore Society* 55(1-4): 6–17, 84–89.

Sutherland, A. (1986). *Gypsies: The Hidden Americans.* Long Grove, IL: Waveland Press. (Originally published, New York: Free Press, 1975.)

Chapter 4

The American *Kris*

To be among a group of Roma is the natural everyday context within which a person lives, learns, and expresses his or her personality; to be among a group of *gadje* is essentially to be alone. Wherever they travel or live, Roma are rarely alone. More often they are surrounded by large numbers of relatives and friends. Only when someone is rejected by the community or when he or she chooses to leave, or when separated from his or her large group of relatives is the person in some sense alone. Loneliness is perhaps the rarest feeling an individual *rom* or *romni* experiences in his or her lifetime.

As might be expected in such a community, visiting and gossip are major pastimes, and it is rare to enter a home that does not have visitors, or to find Roma anywhere who are not discussing the recent events in their own or in other *kumpaniyi.* Just as the Nuer love to talk about cattle (Evans-Pritchard 1940), the Roma love to talk about each other. Of course the frequent marriages, baptisms, parties, feasts, and funerals are always occasions for visiting and gossip.

Besides being a pastime, gossip is also a major form of social control. It is the primary means of pressuring an individual to behave according to Romani morality. Once word gets around that some people consider another person's actions to be immoral, others will not wish to risk contact with the accused and will avoid him or her. Consequently, no individual can afford to ignore anyone's statements concerning his or her reputation no matter how unfounded in fact they may be. Furthermore, an accusation of immoral actions can sully the entire family or *vitsa.* Gossip can make or break a person's reputation, and when it occurs it must be fought immediately. To ignore gossip would be tantamount to admitting guilt. This does not mean there are no curbs on gossiping. One man in Richmond was declared rejected from the community for six months for malicious gossiping.

Costello *Machwaya* women in conversation.

Naturally, visiting and gossip take place among Roma who are living in close proximity—that is, in the same or a nearby *kumpania*. In addition, people in nearby *kumpaniyi* are constantly in touch with each other and maintain an intense system of communication among themselves. They generally know what is happening, what is being talked about, and where people are. During travels, more distant relatives and *vitsi* members are contacted, and every traveler to an area brings news about people in the area they just left. Since there are always people coming and going from the *kumpania*, contact is maintained with many areas of North America. This enhances their sense of solidarity as a people since without communication, they could not maintain their social and moral system.

Of course, not all Roma meet each other in travels, and sometimes it is important to contact relatives or friends who are far away. For example, when there is a serious illness or death, relatives have a duty to come to the side of the stricken person. For these emergencies, the Roma have an amazing system of communication that makes it possible for one person to contact any other in a very short time. Even if the person has deliberately gone into hiding, he or she can often eventually be found. When I did my original fieldwork the telephone was the main means of communication, not just between the Roma but also with key non-Roma who are known to be in touch with a particular community. If they cannot reach someone through other Roma, they contact someone (a social worker, pawnshop operators, undertakers, or police) who is in constant contact with Roma in their area. Today, communication is much easier with many more venues to reach someone. As mentioned in the previous chapter, Roma use email, Facebook, YouTube, and Twitter to keep in touch.

Gossip, visiting, and other forms of communication are informal expressions of solidarity and simultaneously a means of social control. The formal system included, (1) a code of tradition and rules called *romania*, (2) a legal body that makes decisions and enforces the rules *(diwano* and *kris romani)*, and (3) punishment by fine or *marime* to enforce the legal decisions. *Romania* is a set of moral codes and rules of behavior known by all but interpreted primarily by elders. Disagreement about proper behavior takes the form of denying accusations or presenting contradictory statements of fact. Occasionally these customs and rules may be changed over time. At the present time they are going through enormous changes. Conflict over marriages has resulted in "new rules" for elopement, settlement and return of the "marriage payment" or brideprice *(daro),* and being an informant to the police. Choosing one's own marriage partner has now become more common.

Lately these customs are being challenged by two factions of American Roma: First, young people now do not want to accept arranged marriages and want the choice of spouse to be theirs alone. This upsets the system of authority in which parents and grandparents choose a young person's spouse to set up an alliance within the *vitsa* or with other *vitsi*. It also changes the relationship between *Xanamik* who are supposed to have authority over a *bori*. Second, converts to the Roma evangelical churches, which are headed by Roma pastors, challenge the authority of elders as well. These pastors have become authority figures who are highly respected by their congregation. Converts now claim Jesus Christ as the only legitimate authority over them. This means they are in defiance of the authority of elders and even the decisions of the *kris*, which was the ultimate authority in decisions regarding social and moral issues.

The *Kris Romani*

American Roma have their own legal system, or autonomous lawmaking as Weyrauch calls it (Weyrauch 2001), which operates somewhat differently in different Gypsy groups within the United States and abroad. Many Romanies in other countries have no *kris*. Elena Marushiakova and Vesselin Popov

(2007) who studied the presence and absence of the *kris* in the many countries in Central and Eastern Europe concluded that the *kris* is present among the *Vlax*-speaking Roma and most nomadic or formerly nomadic groups. Those Romanies who have been settled for a long time, (e.g., 100 years or more) do not have the *kris*. By Marushiakova and Popov's calculations Romanies without the *kris* are two to three times more numerous than those with the *kris*. Romanies with the *kris* are about 5 to 10 percent of the Romani population. Economic nomadism seems to be an essential element for retaining the *kris*.

In both the United States and in the communities in Europe who have the *kris,* there are specific kinds of cases that go to the *kris:* disputes over monetary debts or economic territories between two *vitsi,* family disputes about a failed marriage and refusal to return a portion of the marriage payment, or an accusation of a serious a breach of morality. Violent crimes and murder are considered so heinous, they are not brought to the *kris* and are left to the police and American courts to handle. In cases of violence and fraud (which the police unfortunately and prejudicially call "Gypsy Crimes") that go to American courts, relatives of the accused do not want to ruin their standing in the community by supporting their accused relative; therefore, they are unlikely to cooperate or help the relative's defense attorneys. Neither defense nor prosecuting attorneys know of, or care about, the parallel authority of the *kris* and recognize no role for the *kris* in the totality of the formal US legal process. For the Roma, however, the opinion of the other Roma and the *kris* is the central question at stake.

There is no term in English equivalent to the *kris* or the decision-making body. But it is based on the concept of the consensus of the community's judgment on an individual. The existence of parallel legal systems is not unique to the Roma. American Indians have their own courts based on their own traditions and sometimes federal courts have allowed them to carry out a punishment from their traditions. In Muslim countries or among Muslim immigrants sharia law, a legal code based on the Quran and other Islamic scripture (Lipka 2015), often conflicts with the legal codes of the governing state or country. The difference between sharia law and the *kris romani* is that the sharia law has a written, coded set of practices.

In the United States the *kris romani* consists of a selected number of *rom* and a *krisitori,* a *rom* who is known to be honest and wise and will listen to the arguments from all sides of the conflict and then decide the guilt or innocence and penalty for a member of the Roma community who has committed an offense against other Roma. The *rom* are not judges, but respected men known for their fair and impartial judgment who listen to all parties and come to an agreement by consensus about a case. The *krisitori* should not be from either party in the dispute, rather someone from a *vitsa* or *kumpania* close by. Their decision is final, and the accused pledges to accept it before the *kris* convenes. Not to accept the decision would be to tantamount to rejecting *romania*. Punishment includes fines, being declared *bolime* (that is "black-balled" or declared morally unclean—*marime),* to be denied physical contact and social intercourse with one's own people, and therefore to be forced to live among the *gadje. Romania* is social life; *marime* is social death.

The outcome is a resolution, usually a fine and/or being shunned for a specific period of time. A *marime* decision meant no Roma could meet with the shunned person and particularly could not eat with that person. The family of the *marime* had to abide by the decision or they, too, would become *marime,* but all Roma would also do so for fear of being seen as *marime* as well. The *kris* worked well as long as everyone involved accepted the validity and judgment of the *kris*. During my fieldwork, there were several *kris,* and I did not hear of anyone ignoring the *kris* decision.

Many of the disputes arising from a marriage may be taken to the *kris romani* for resolution. This is the only way to officially dissolve a marriage. Since the *daro* (the payment of the groom's family to the bride's family) is still practiced, a marriage dispute (between the two families) has to be resolved with the return of a portion of the *daro* to the groom's family. If the bride was a virgin at marriage, the *daro* is a considerable amount of money, but in a dissolution of the marriage, the bride is no longer a virgin and therefore not all the *daro* is returned.

The following is a verbatim account of a *kris* from John Marks. Keep in mind that I only have his version of the *kris,* and it is a one-sided opinion of what happened. It gives an idea of the complexity and pain of the dissolution of a marriage and the reasons why young people are rebelling against this system.

The *Kris* as It Once Was

Kris romani between *Xanamik* John Marks and Stevan Costello: taped verbatim from John Marks:

> *I am going to talk about a Gypsy trial. Now this story is based on a true trial, on a Gypsy trial which consists of judge and juries on a Gypsy marriage case which includes a divorce and a settlement, not between bride and*

groom but between the father of the son and the father of the daughter. Now this is a case between John Marks[1] and the family of Stevan, who were engaged in a marriage between my son and Stevan who has a daughter that I wanted for a daughter-in-law. Now we arranged for a marriage between the parents of the bride and groom which is a tradition in the way the Gypsies go about marrying their son or daughter. Now the girl's father, Stevan, offered to marry his daughter to be the wife to my son, Danny. We agreed on a price to be paid the girl's father for her hand in marriage to my son. And some time after the wedding my son and his bride did not get along.

It is more enjoyable to get a daughter-in-law from a cousin because there's been lots of dirty business. A man makes money giving a daughter-in-law by marrying her several times to different people. He does this by giving her for six months, then builds up evidence such as they beat her or her father-in-law made a pass at her, then her father takes her back and does not return the money. So it used to be you got a daughter-in-law from a different vitsa, but now it is better to get one in the family.

When I got one for Danny she wouldn't sleep with him as a wife, only as a sister. Her father had put her up to it. So I got in touch with her father and said I wanted my money back. He said no, that I was trying to make love to my daughter-in-law, and he made his mistake when he said that. Now I knew that she had committed a crime before and was wanted for picking a man's pocket of $300. I went to the sheriff there and said that I would bring her in if he would bring her father down and cause him a lot of trouble and money. I drove her down to the sheriff because he agreed, and she was arrested and spent time in jail until her father posted bond. They fought the case on several occasions. Her father was in Reno and I had him picked up over there, and he had to pay bond to get out. I also had her arrested on charges in Fort Worth. She had an uncle in Beaumont who thought he could handle everything I did. They put her in the hospital on false charges (and I told the judge that) while trial had been delayed. He was furious that they had tried to make a fool out of him and sent two men down to see if she was really ill, and if not, to escort her to the trial. All this made a fool out of her father and her uncle. I had things pretty well arranged in Weatherford, Texas, and she had to plead guilty and was given a five-year sentence on probation. We still had to have a Gypsy hearing to settle our differences. They tried to blackmail me in the same way but they had nothing on me so they failed.

Now this takes us months later to New Orleans to a Gypsy trial. The Stevan family did not want to meet in Texas figuring that I was too powerful in Texas, and I had all my friends here in Texas, and they wanted a Gypsy trial by other members of the Gypsies from all parts of the United States. And that way I had to go to New Orleans for this trial to satisfy the company [kumpa-

nia] *the* [Roma] *public. In New Orleans there was about five hundred Gypsies there for this trial. So between John Marks and Stevan money-wise we arranged for a hall where the public can gather and listen to both sides of the story. And besides this would be the best way to settle the matter. We rented this hall, and we set a date the following couple of days to give everybody a time and chance to be there. The majority of the Gypsies was gathered at this hall; then they started picking out a judge and juries, which consisted out of different vitsi which is called "generation" and families. This went on for several hours. There were two judges and twenty-five jurors at this particular trial. It doesn't ordinarily take more than one judge and ten or twelve jurors, but in this particular case, there was a lot of conflict. One judge was Alex Tan of Chicago, and one judge was Sonny Mitchell from Alabama. They are known to be honest and are well respected among the Gypsies for their honesty. At this trial, John Marks who is the father of Danny, the groom's father, was asked to take the stand and tell his story to the public, to the best of his knowledge. This took another couple of hours. Then Stevan was called to the witness stand. He gave his testimony to the judges and the jury and the public. His story was that my son wasn't old enough for his daughter. My son at the time was fifteen years old, and his daughter was twenty.*

Now I don't know where to go from there. All right. They're going to hang me for this. He said his daughter's complaint to him was that John Marks had bossed her a great deal in the period she was married to my son. Also, my wife disagreed to her behavior and to her standards as a daughter-in-law. It was true, she wanted it that way. She was trying to make everything the opposite for us. It was all a set-up by her father and his brothers. He also accused me of trying to make love to his daughter which was my daughter-in-law. Now that accusation would condemn any Gypsy to a judge and jury if his story was true. He also accused the Boy's father of not giving them a large sum of money and setting them up on their own. But it was not promised as far as that goes. They were not living with us. I had bought them a trailer, a nice sixteen-foot house trailer, and he had his own car, and he had his own money that I gave him. So that wasn't true.

Then the judge and jury went to a secluded part of this hall to decide the true story of this case. They reviewed both sides of the story and found John Marks innocent of all the accusations. They found Stevan to be a fraud and to be in the business of making money on his daughter by marrying her at one place for three or four thousand dollars, getting her back and giving no money back, turning around and remarrying her again for a large sum of money and keeping the money again. So in review of the case they also reviewed the side of John Marks who had had this trial before a Gypsy court because he started his arrest on Stevan and his family to get even with them *for the heartache he had caused his family. He would have been found to receive all his money from the Stevan family, but because of John Marks and the rage of madness which followed when he knew that he was being took by the Stevan family and also made a fool of—he was not really blamed for the action he took for the past several months—therefore, the juries agreed that the Marks family receive $2000 on refund. But through their conversation in the jury box they knew that the Stevan family did not have that kind of money, and the juries also knew that if they did not come to some decision where this case be settled at this time that this trouble could last indefinitely between the Marks and Stevan's family. Therefore, they agreed (along with the judges) to let Stevan pay $1000 and call it a final settlement on a divorce for both sides, the bride and groom. When the jury and the judges came back to the stand, they explained the money situation to the Marks family, and to show respect to the public they asked John Marks if he would do the public a favor and accept the decision of this court even though it wasn't quite fair to the Marks. But to avoid more trouble in the future, they had to come to this conclusion on account of the Stevan family, outside of this few thousand dollars they received for their daughter, they have lived from day to day not knowing the value of money, and they were actually not having more than a few hundred dollars at any one time. The Marks family wanted to get away from all this trouble and get their son properly married to some other woman, and they had to come to some conclusion at this time, so they did accept the court's verdict and gave their word that they would accept all responsibility of not creating any more trouble in the future. Stevan in return took the stand in his behalf and said that he would need three months to raise the thousand dollars, and at the end of three months he would send the money to John Marks. The court was asked if John Marks would accept Stevan's extension. He refused. The only way the Marks would accept such an extension was to have three people that was reliable to back Stevan as security so that Stevan would not double-cross John Marks at the end of the three months. So the court agreed to decide who would be the three men who would stand fully responsible for the thousand dollars in such a case. In another hour or so they came up with Sonny Mitchell as one respectable and reliable person and Alex Tan and Grover Marks. They are more or less my friends, and they accepted the responsibility and accepted the security that the money will be paid by the Stevan's, and they gave their word to the court that if the Stevan's side did not come across at the end of the three months with the thousand dollars that between Sonny Mitchell, Alex Tan, and Grover Marks, that I was guaranteed my money from them regardless.*

Ninety per cent of the time, there is no welshing. Once any family or any person, even without a "background," gives his word to the public, they gen-

erally live up to it. But in this case, at the end of the three months, the Stevan family was in Wichita, Kansas, and John Marks contacted them for his thousand dollars. Then Stevan said that his daughter wanted to come back and remarry my son, and he was afraid to give me the $1000 because his daughter might elope with my son. I tried to explain to Stevan that we did not want his daughter, that my son did not want his daughter, there was no possible chance of the kids getting back together. Now or ever. That this was another way of Stevan to try to release the people that was responsible in the case and swindle me out of my thousand dollars which I had coming. I had a pretty good idea he was going to do that. I immediately got in touch with Sonny Mitchell from Alabama and explained to him what Stevan was trying to pull. And I insisted on my money. He was one of the responsible persons to give me my money. In return, Sonny Mitchell from Alabama asked me if I could meet him by the following morning in Wichita, Kansas, and if I would extend him that much time to see if he could get the money himself from Stevan instead of involving Alex Tan and Grover Marks and a further ordeal. But this was further expense to me so I went prepared. I got hold of six of my best muscle men of the family and got in the car, and we arrived in Wichita. The reason I gathered six of the Marks muscle boys was that Stevan (and there was a couple of his brothers in Wichita) himself weighed about 400 lb. He was a huge man. I knew there was gonna be a fight, and I went prepared for it. We arrived in Wichita and gathered at George Evans' home, who is a personal friend of the Marks. Sonny Mitchell arrived and if it wasn't for George Evans and his boys there would have been a large fight at this time because Stevan insisted that he could not give the money. Sonny told him that he promised the public that he would have to return that money. This went on for two days. Arguments were very hot. A lot of harsh words was relayed between the Marks and Stevan family. Finally after two days of a talking battle, Stevan did come up with the $1000 to Sonny Mitchell in return who did give the money to John Marks.

Well he was a disgrace to the Gypsy tribe already when he refused, when he welshed on a promise that he gave his word, that he said in the Gypsy trial in New Orleans that he would give a $1000 which John Marks had coming. And of course like we mentioned before, Stevan was a very dirty man. In Wichita he was more or less forced to give the money up to the public which he did, you know what I mean, after a long ordeal and so forth. I never met him again. I have no relationships with him. My boy is married now. He has two fine daughters. He has a good wife. The first marriage of my son cost me about $15,000 which I carried to experience. There is no need to hold a grudge because it would just mean more trouble in the future. I just forgot about it.

You see, that's why any one person, whether he is a Costello or a Mitchell, or an Evans, or a Stevenson, he tries to stay as close in the family as he can, not for the money but it has happened in the past where if you receive a daughter-in-law from far off away from the family, nine times out of ten that marriage doesn't last. Besides you might hurt your son or your daughter whichever might be implicated. The heartbreak, the ordeal, for your son— suppose he fell in love with this woman and for no reason at all his home is broken up through his father-in-law—he would feel very hurt. If a daughter got married, and the fathers-in-law broke up her home, and they were so strange, so strangers and so far apart that they could not get together and talk about this marriage like friends and relatives. If they were strangers, that home would have a poor chance of getting back together even though the kids are in love and do not want their home broken. But by Gypsy laws and traditions that home is broken. If the father-in-law breaks it up there is not much the kids can do about it unless in a few cases in the past the kids did elope, run away with one another, and got lost as long as a year from both parents from both sides and made a go of their marriage.

The *Kris* Today

The above narrative, recorded in Fort Worth, Texas, illustrates the way the *kris* previously worked, and the pressure on every *rom* to agree on the verdict of the *kris*. It also shows that it was hard to enforce a verdict. Today, it is even more difficult. In addition to the lack of gatherings of a wider number of *vitsi* other than in the Roma churches, there are other indications of a considerably weakened *kris*.

First, besides the *kris* no longer representing several groups, there has been an influx of immigrant Roma into the United States who come from groups that do not practice the *kris* and who do not recognize the authority of the *kris* to handle internal conflict.

Second, the *kris* does not deal with murder, armed robbery, or assault of a non-Gypsy (Weyrauch 2001) so Roma themselves may turn to the American legal system to take care of the punishment—removal of the guilty from the Roma community by the judicial body's ruling of imprisonment or death.

Third, it has become common for younger generations of Roma to use American courts to solve internal problems that in the past would have been handled by the *kris*. A recent territorial dispute among the Stevens and Merino *vitsi* in wealthy Newport Beach, California, is an example of a dispute over economic resources that would normally be handled by the *kris*. Newport Beach has several locations of lucrative fortune-telling establishments. In addition to charging a handsome fee for telling someone's fortune, fortune-tellers have expanded their practice to include drawing a picture of the client's soul for $50. These are both legal transactions. Competition for these fortune-telling locations is fierce, with one family trying to keep another family from opening competing locations. Instead of going to a *kris* to resolve this problem, they have resorted to physical fights. This has resulted in arrests, restraining orders on each other, and a case in an American court. According to Ian Hancock, "that the dispute wound up in court reflects an erosion of tradition among the Gypsies" (Kahn 2007).

Ian Hancock described what is happening to the *kris* in the following paraphrase of personal communication from him: According to Hancock:

> *The strength of the* kris *is based on the strength of the consensus among different groups about correct ways of being, morality, and how to solve economic differences. Today there are fewer large gatherings of different* Romanies *in the community or area. People can communicate easily by email, cell phone and keep in touch with each other when on the move in ways they never could. They are observing the Slavic calendar less and giving more importance to American holidays such as Thanksgiving, Christmas and July 4th. They watch more TV and use the Internet and gather mostly in groups of extended families. In these gatherings there is less representation from a broad spectrum of* vitsi *and larger groups. The* kris *used to crosscut many* vitsi/natsia, *but since there are fewer and fewer gatherings that do that, there are less* rom *for the* kris *to draw from. The* kris *is no longer representative of several groups and therefore its authority to enforce its rulings is weakened. If it is mainly two families from two* vitsi; vitsa *members side with their family member, and there is not a larger contingency of* Roma *to exert authority over the* vitsa.*
>
> *The vacuum left by a less-effective* kris *has been filled somewhat by the Sunday meetings of Roma in a Roma evangelical church. On Sundays Roma from many different groups who have converted to evangelical religions come together under the umbrella of the church. Sunday is one of the few times and church one of the few places where large gatherings of Roma can exert moral pressure on others. The Machwaya, who mostly have not become evangelicals and still practice a form of Orthodox Christianity without a Roma church, still have the* kris *as I have described it. But Roma in the evangelical Roma church have moved away from the* kris.

In the next chapter I discuss different understandings of identity between the Roma and American society and law. I illustrate these differences in a case that took place in Minnesota for which I was appointed an expert witness for the defense but actually took the role as a cultural broker between Roma law and American law.

1. What kind of disputes are handled by the *kris,* and which are not?
2. What is the role of gossip in Romani culture? What is the "Gypsy hotline" in Los Angeles?
3. How has Dr. Ian Hancock, a Romani, described the changes in Romani cultural practices recently? Are these changes likely to indicate assimilation into American culture?
4. What information about the *kris* and cultural practices among the Roma do you learn from the testimony of John Marks?

References

Evans-Pritchard, E. E. (1940). *The Nuer.* Oxford: Oxford University Press.

Kahn, J. (2007, December 6). "Gypsy Wars in Newport Beach." *OC Weekly.* Retrieved from http://www.ocweekly.com/news/gypsy-wars-in-newport-beach-6459217.

Lipka, M. (2015, December 7). "Muslims and Islam: Key Findings in the U.S. and around the World." *Pew Research Center.* Retrieved from http://www.pewresearch.org/fact-tank/2015/12/07/muslims-and-islam-key-findings-in-the-u-s-and-around-the-world/.

Marushiakova, E. and Popov, V. (2007). "The Gypsy Court in Eastern Europe." *Romani Studies* 17: 67–101.

Weyrauch, W. O. (2001). *Gypsy Law: Romani Legal Traditions and Culture.* Berkeley: University of California Press.

Chapter 5

Roma Identities and American Identities

Fundamental differences between sedentary societies and traveling societies frequently lead to conflict between them. Conflicts stem from the interests vested in the basic social and legal forms of societies organized around individuals being in a fixed place versus the interests of societies organized around the flexibility of being able to move from place to place. In *sedentary* societies (which developed historically with agriculture), each person has an official and personal identity linked to a fixed abode (an address), a name (a legal name), and often documents of proof of identity (birth certificate, identity card, driver's license, passport, etc.). In traveling societies, individuals do not have a fixed abode, but work and live within a broad territory; they may have several names or identities suitable for each location within which they work, and their identity is corporate, that is, based on that which is fixed in their lives: membership in a broad kin group within which they are born or married. Their relationship with the state is therefore often problematic, and government officials frequently view traveling peoples as a threat to the state. People who are not easily located are hard to control.

The global history of the relationships between emerging states and traveling peoples, often called nomadic people in the anthropological literature, (for example, Indians in the US, Bedouins in Arabia, or Maasi in Kenya), is commonly a history of discrimination, persecution, violence, forced assimilation, or containment on reservations. The Roma are a people with such a history. Persecuted with various degrees of harshness throughout the last millennium during their movement west from Northern India, they have been vilified, subject to laws targeting their traveling ways, forcibly evicted from towns (England, France, US), expelled *en masse* from the state (present-day Germany, Italy, and France), enslaved (Romania), imprisoned and exterminated (Hitler's Germany), and forced to settle (Soviet Union and Eastern bloc states). Some have stayed in one place (the Spanish *Kale* and Romanian Roma being prominent examples), but many have continued to pursue a traveling life and culture based on large kin groups moving around in pursuit of a living.

As I have mentioned, there are many different groups in the United States subdivided loosely into nations (or tribes) of which two, the *Kalderasha* and the *Machwaya,* are predominant. These nations are further subdivided into large extended kin groups known as *vitsiya* (pl.). The *vitsa* is the primary basis of identity for an individual: the source of a man or woman's personal name, family name, and social status. Significant relationships throughout life are based on membership in a *vitsa*. There are, of course, nuances and complications in this system (for example, women over time may take on the identity of their husband's *vitsa),* but in basic terms identity is fixed by birth in a kin group, and personal identity is established and determined by that membership.

In the United States, on the whole, Roma enjoy more human rights and suffer less persecution than they do in Europe. In the early part of this century, when Gypsies migrated in large numbers from the East Coast of the United States to the West Coast, Gypsies were feared and despised and often

Ian Hancock with Roma from various groups.

arrested for purportedly stealing children (a myth that has amazingly persisted to this day). They were run out of town amid wild rumors and warnings to the local citizenry published in local papers. Today, however, both the legal system and the attitudes of people toward ethnic minorities present a much improved picture, improved but not resolved. To illustrate, the rest of this chapter looks at an encounter between a young *rom* and federal law, an encounter that reveals the more subtle problems experienced by traveling Roma living in a sedentary society.

United States v. Nicholas

In the fall of 1991, a 19-year-old *rom*, Sonny Nicholas, was convicted of the crime of using a Social Security number that belonged to his five-year-old nephew. He subsequently served a prison term of six months. The conviction was based on a law making the use of another's Social Security number a federal felony. This law was intended primarily to help with the prosecution of major drug crime syndicates and others who falsify Social Security numbers in order to commit serious crimes. However, as is sometimes the case, a law made for one set of purposes has an unintended impact on a particular ethnic or minority or group.

The case came to my attention when I was asked by the defense to be an "expert witness" on Roma culture. Arguments in the case concentrated on three lines of reasoning: (1) the Social Security law unfairly singled out Roma for punishment; (2) there was no intent to commit a crime; and (3) in using the Social Security numbers of relatives, Roma are following a cultural tradition based on the idea of a kin group as a corporate group. This tradition helped them to remain anonymous and separate from non-Gypsy society and is part of their strategy to survive in sedentary societies.

Background of the Case

Sonny Nicholas (S.N.) came to St. Paul, Minnesota, from Los Angeles with his brothers and, using the Social Security number of his five-year-old nephew, obtained credit to purchase a car at a local dealership. Noting the birth date associated with the Social Security number, a few days later the car dealership asked him to return the car. When S.N. returned the car to the dealership, he was arrested on the felony charge of using a false Social Security number. The police searched his apartment and found lists of names, addresses, and Social Security numbers, leading to suspicion of an organized crime ring.

In *United States v. Nicholas,* it was "alleged that the defendant, S.N., while in the process of obtaining a new Ford Mustang from a car dealership, used a Social Security number that was not his own with intent to deceive." Under statute 42 U.S.C. 408 (g) (2), "a person who, with intent to deceive, falsely represents his or her number to obtain something of value or for any other purpose, is a felon."

The defense lawyer noted that there was no allegation of attempted theft. The focus of the charging statute was false representation of numbers. He argued that the "underlying purpose which motivates a person to falsely represent his or her number may be an essentially innocent purpose, but the statute, at least as it has been interpreted, does not appear to impose a burden of proof as to wrongful purpose. The statute punishes the means (false number) which a person may employ to achieve any number of ends and it punishes those means as a felony."

Furthermore, he argued that the statute's failure to address the purpose to which false credentials are used is a serious flaw in the law and may punish those who would use the number for petty misconduct at a felony level crime. He suggested there is potential for discriminatory impact on Roma who use each other's credentials to conceal themselves from mainstream society. For example, a Roma household may obtain a telephone by providing a relative's Social Security number, and even if they pay the telephone bill without fail for years, they are felons under this law. In this case, S.N. not only made the payments for his car, but he returned it when he was questioned. Nevertheless, he was still a felon under this law.

The defense lawyer argued that the law is objectionable for two reasons. First, the law's disproportionate impact on the Roma is objectionable under the equal protection guarantees in the Fifth Amendment of the US Constitution. The law denies Roma equal protection by irrationally and disproportionately punishing at the felony level certain traditional Roma conduct which causes no positive injury to anyone. As evidence for this case he called on material from my book, *Gypsies, the Hidden Americans* (Sutherland 1986 [1975]), for testimony that Roma routinely use a *vitsa* member's Social Security number to acquire credit but do pay their bills and are available for repossession of the purchases in case of default of payment. They obtain phone service, buy houses and cars and other household items on credit, and have a record of payment that is probably better than that of the general population. They do this primarily to remain unknown by mainstream society, rather than to cause loss or injury to any person.

Second, the proceeding conflicted with a Supreme Court decision that requires the government to prove felonious intent when it seeks to punish a person for wrongful acquisition of another's property. The defense lawyer argued that S.N. used another relative's Social Security number because of a Roma tradition to remain anonymous and because his own number had been used by his uncles and others.

The federal prosecutor, on the other hand, argued that there was a "ring" of Roma in the area, with whom Sonny Nicholas was associated. At Sonny Nicholas' residence, a number of credentials and Social Security numbers used to obtain cars were found. Some of these cars were still missing at the time of the trial. In other words, there was evidence that false identity had been used recently in the area to commit thefts. However, Sonny Nicholas himself had not stolen anything and was not being accused of stealing, only of using a false Social Security number.

Because of the suspicion of a "ring of car thieves" in the area, the prosecution hoped to use the threat of prosecution against Sonny Nicholas, the only *rom* they were able to arrest, to plea bargain for information regarding the other people involved in the alleged ring. These other people had disappeared immediately after Sonny Nicholas was arrested.

One of the problems in the case was that both the prosecution and the defense had difficulty understanding the situation they faced. Neither could establish complete and accurate information on Sonny Nicholas, beginning with his "real" name, which they never did determine correctly. Although I explained the Roma practice of using many "American" names but only one Roma name, neither the prosecution nor the defense was satisfied with a Roma name. For example, the Roma name, of *o Spiro le Stevanosko* (or Spiro, the son of Stevan) uses the noun declension characteristic of the Sanskrit- rooted language and does not employ a surname. Spiro's identity can be pinned down by finding out what *vitsa* he belongs to so that he will not be mixed up with any other *Spiro le Stevanoskos.* The Spiro of our example is a *Kashtare,* which is part of a larger "nation" of Roma or *natsia* called *Kalderasha* (coppersmiths). For his "American" names he may take any of a number of American names used by his relatives such as Spiro Costello, John Costello, John Marks, John Miller, Spiro John, or Spiro Miller. His nickname is Rattlesnake Pete.

Also, neither the defense nor the prosecution was able to deal with two issues. First, Roma, organized around traditions suitable for a nomadic people, frequently borrow each other's "American" names and Social Security numbers, viewing them as a kind of corporate property of their kin group.

Second, Roma families who move around the country on a regular basis often lack official birth certificates and must somehow find the *romni* midwife to write out one or get baptismal certificates to use for identification purposes to obtain a Social Security number, enter school, or apply for a driver's license.

Anthropologist as Cultural Broker

Sonny Nicholas' defense attorney contacted me after reading my book, *Gypsies, the Hidden Americans* (Sutherland 1986 [1975]) where he learned that his confusion about Sonny Nicholas was helped by understanding something about the Roma. For his case he needed to determine if Sonny Nicholas really was a Roma, find out his name and circumstances, and get some cultural information that would help him with his case (such as the use of Social Security numbers by Roma).

Consequently, one cold fall day in Minnesota, I drove up to the federal prison, one and a half hours from St. Paul, to meet with Sonny Nicholas. He was a thin young man, scared and nervous, in perpetual fear of becoming unclean from contact with non-Roma, and suffering from the effects of several months of being isolated from his people. The limited telephone calls allowed him to talk with his family, but his main contact was with a non-Gypsy woman with whom one of his relatives lived. She was his link between the world he had known and the non-Gypsy world, and hers was the only "American" household he had been in before prison.

Since my primary task was to determine if he was a Roma, first I talked to him about his relatives in Los Angeles and his *vitsa* and tried to establish what families in the *vitsa* I personally knew. This exchange of information about *vitsa* and Roma of mutual acquaintance is a normal one between Roma. The purpose is to establish a link between two persons meeting for the first time.

To help the defense collect accurate information on the facts of the case, I asked him what had happened and why he was in Minnesota. He talked about a seasonal expedition he and his brothers and cousins make to Minnesota to buy and sell cars and fix fenders before winter arrives. Seasonal mobility is part of the traveling culture they have. He claimed not to know where his brothers and cousins had gone or how he got into his present predicament. He was somewhat perplexed at being arrested since he had stolen nothing, and he certainly did not understand the law, fairly recent at the time, under which he was charged.

Somewhat frustrated with efforts to facilitate communication between Sonny and his defense lawyer, I sought to take action on his conditions in prison. When I met him, Sonny had lost 15 pounds in the month that he was in federal prison and was suffering demonstrable distress and nervousness. Like many other prisoners, he was distressed because he was incarcerated for the first time in his life. He was also fearful of the other prisoners and worried about his safety while in prison.

But as a Roma he had two serious concerns particular to his culture. While in prison he was cut off from his culture and people without any possibility of face-to-face contact. Within his own culture's legal system (the *kris*), the most severe punishment imposed upon a Roma who has transgressed an important code of conduct is to be declared *marime* by the group for a specified period of time. As mentioned previously, *marime* denies the individual access to all other Roma (including family) except by telephone and is viewed both as a kind of solitary confinement as well as a condition of constant moral impurity until readmission to the group.

In addition, confinement in prison meant he had to worry about becoming defiled *(marime)* through the food, close physical contact with non-Gypsies, and exposure to prison germs. He was worried that if he ate food prepared by non-Gypsies who do not follow rules of cleanliness considered essential in the Roma culture, he would become *marime*. To avoid this fate, he refused prison food in the hope that when he was released from prison he would be able to return to his family without a period of physical exile.

Although there was no remedy for his close physical contact with non-Gypsies and exposure to prison germs, the food problem was relatively simple to ameliorate. I arranged for his lawyer to provide him with money to buy food from the concession because it is packaged and considered "untouched" by non-Gypsies and therefore considered clean by Roma standards. He bought milk in cartons, candy bars and soft drinks, and other packaged foods that, though they may not have provided balanced nutrition, at least were not defiling and kept him from starvation. Because I presented these food choices as part of their religion, the authorities were very willing to comply.

A further complicating factor for Sonny was that he spoke English as a second language. His ability to read was rudimentary, thus straining his grasp of his defense. Even though his limited English made it difficult for him to follow his own trial, the court did not provide a translator.

The Trial

The trial, held in the United States District Court of Minnesota, centered around the constitutionality of a law that unfairly targets a particular ethnic group and the question of intent to commit a crime. My testimony was intended to establish that Roma may use a relative's identification for a number of cultural reasons that may have no connection with any intent to commit a crime. For a traditionally nomadic group with pariah status in the wider society and a pattern of secretiveness and autonomy, the argument went, concealing identity is a long-established pattern. This pattern, widespread among all Roma groups in Eastern Europe, Western Europe, Russia, Latin America, and the United States, is a mechanism the Roma developed over centuries to protect themselves from a wider society that has persecuted them, moved them on, and treated them as parasites.

Both historical and current examples of persecution were presented. For, example, the German government had paid large sums to Romania to take back Roma refugees. The persecution of Roma in the Holocaust, in medieval Europe, and in the early part of the 20th century in the United States has been well documented. Current events in Eastern Europe showed a resurgence of extreme prejudice against Roma. Interviews in *New York Times* articles showed a hatred of Roma so deep that some people talked of extermination (Kamm 1993a, 1993b). Because of the history of violence against them, Roma developed elaborate mechanisms of secrecy and hid their identity in order to survive. I argued that they have little motivation to change a pattern that has stood them in good stead for so many centuries.

An additional complication for Sonny was the question of identification from photographs. Here we came up against the age-old problem of members from one culture and race having trouble identifying individuals from another culture and race. In simple terms, to many non-Roma, all Roma look alike. Part of the case involved clearing up erroneous identification of Sonny in photos provided by the prosecution, most of which were photos of other people.

The purpose of my testimony was to establish that S.N. was a Roma and that Roma often use many names and identification documents without intent to defraud. They do so because as members of a *vitsa,* identification is corporate in nature. Members of the group have access to property owned by other members of the group. That property includes forms of identification.

I was also asked to testify regarding my own personal experience with discrimination against Roma by the Minneapolis Police Department. This occurred during a talk I gave to some 20 police officers to help them understand Roma culture. When I spoke about the strong sense of family and community among the Roma, in particular how important their children are, one officer suggested that since their main problem is how to detain Roma long enough to prosecute them, removing Roma children from their homes on any pretext would be an effective way to keep the parents in town!

Prejudice against Roma often goes unrecognized even by normally culturally and racially sensitive people. The assistant district attorney prosecuting Sonny offered me an article that he used to understand the Roma, entitled "GYP-sies, the People and Their Criminal Propensity" (Getsay 1982), of which the very title is pejorative. This inflammatory article quotes extensively from my book, including the fact that they have several names and that the same or similar non-Roma names are used over and over. Having many "aliases" was a kind of proof of criminality. The article concentrates on "criminal" behavior and never mentions the possibility that there are Roma who may not engage in criminal activities. In one section, there are quotes from my book on the ways Roma deal with the welfare bureaucracy placed under the title, "Welfare Fraud," although by far most of the practices I described were legal. The conclusion in the article is representative of the tone of the article: "Officers should not be misled into thinking these people are not organized. They are indeed organized and operate under established rules of behavior, including those that govern marriage, living quarters, child rearing, the division of money and participation in criminal acts" (Getsay 1982). These are highly inflammatory statements. Roma have a culture, history, language, and social structure, but that fact is distorted to imply that their social organization is partly for the purpose of facilitating criminal behavior. The prosecution saw their culture as a "criminal" culture, a viewpoint that Roma have been fighting for hundreds of years and still combat in their relations with law enforcement and the criminal justice system.

The American law enforcement and legal systems are, of course, not the only systems to single out Roma as a criminal culture, unworthy of basic respect. Indeed, I have personally witnessed far worse examples of legal injustices and police brutality against Roma. In Stara Zagora, Bulgarian police broke up community gatherings in a public park and brutally beat several men, including one man in his 70s. Roma informants and a Bulgarian ethnographer confirmed that such treatment is so commonplace that the Roma have come to expect it. In Budapest, Hungary, police stood by while a mob of skinheads ransacked an apartment house occupied by Roma and beat several occupants, including women, who were later hospitalized. I have not heard of such instances of brutality by the police in major American cities, but they do train their officers to regard the Roma as an organized criminal culture, a "poor man's mafia." This practice has far-reaching implications for the position of Roma in relation to the US judicial system.

In spite of the best efforts of Sonny's attorney and my testimony that use of a nephew's Social Security number did not necessarily indicate intent to commit a crime, he was convicted of illegally using a Social Security number and served six months in federal prison.

Social Anthropology: Examining Cultural Differences in Legal Systems

The analysis of an event such as a trial, especially an event that brings to the fore cultural differences, can be instructive for both cultures (Clifford 1988). Understanding differences does not necessarily resolve conflict, but it can lead to a more humanitarian application of the law to different cultures. The United States, a country based on immigration and diversity, is in no position to ignore the cultural foundations of different ethnic groups. Of course, different cultures in the United States are not exempt from a law because it is contrary to custom. However, the more aware the legal system is of cultural histories and customs, the greater its capacity for justice. Justice is particularly difficult for the Roma to obtain in American courts because of three mitigating circumstances.

First is the question of the cultural conflict between a historically nomadic group and the state bureaucracy of settled people. Identification, a serious legal issue in a bureaucratic society composed of people with fixed abodes and a written language, has virtually no meaning for the nomadic Roma who consider descent and extended family ties the defining factor for identification.

Second is the conflict between Roma religious rules regarding ritual pollution and jail or prison regulations. The Roma avoid situations, such as a job or jail, that require them to be in prolonged contact with non-Gypsies. Jail or prison presents special problems because the Roma can become *marime*. The psychological trauma that results from isolation from their community is compounded if they then emerge from jail and have to undergo a *kris* that may result in further isolation from relatives because of becoming *marime* in jail.

Finally, this case illustrates a cultural clash between the Roma value of corporate kinship and the American value of individual rights. The rights and status of an individual *rom* or *romni* is directly linked to his or her membership in the *vitsa*. Furthermore, the status of all members of the *vitsa* is affected by the behavior of each individual *vitsa* member. Since they are so intricately linked, reciprocity between *vitsi* members is expected. Members of a *vitsa* and family share economic resources, stay in each other's homes, help each other in work and preparation of rituals, loan each other cars, information, identification, and money. They also share the shame of immoral or incorrect behavior by one member and the stigma *(marime)* attached to going to jail. For the Roma, the American ideal of each individual having only one name, one social security number, or a reputation based entirely on their own behavior is contrary to their experience and culture.

Thus, when Roma get out of jail or prison, they must submit to another trial, a *kris,* which is held by their own people, to "reinstate" a person. Ian Hancock has reported that a *kris* held for a family some months ago in Chattanooga resulted in reinstatement after a specified period of *marime.* Because the case involved rape and incest, several people did not honor the reinstatement, although such a decision should be binding. The severity of the crime may have had an influence on people's feelings about reinstatement (personal communication).

The most notorious California figure to serve time in prison was Barbara Miller, convicted of fraud in the 1970s, with the help of other Roma who hoped to break her control over fortune-telling in San Francisco (Miller 2010). She had no *kris* when she returned from prison; however, she did not make an appearance with other Roma for about five years after her release. She also was ostracized by some Roma for many years afterward. Although there is no rule that requires someone coming out of prison to be cleared by a *kris,* some people are isolated automatically if the crime is considered serious. For example, a Roma family in Hawaii that had committed a murder had not been welcome at any *Machwaya* Roma event for some time, and it was generally agreed that they would not dare show up. The isolation constitutes a penalty. A *kris* would be appropriate if the criminal gets another Roma in trouble or causes so much trouble with the police that they bring the law down on other Roma in the area. In these cases, the *kris* is needed to determine a fine or the length of time a person is blackballed *(bolime).*

Another case in San Francisco involved a girl who ran away from her parents to join the Job Corps, an organization that to many Roma resembles prison. After a few lonely months she called home, and her parents immediately brought her back. A *kris,* composed of all the adult men in the vicinity, was assembled in a park in the center of town. Women were present to comment, but they did not directly take part in the proceedings. They passed around documents that the girl's mother had obtained with the help of their social worker. Three documents were required: a gynecological exam to determine that she did not have venereal disease, a statement from a psychiatrist that she was sane (he was instructed by her mother to "fix her mind so she would not do it again"), and an affidavit from the social worker that the Job Corps was not a prison. The *kris* accepted all three documents as valid, and the verdict was one month *marime,* after which the girl was welcomed back into the community and quickly married to a *rom* chosen by her parents.

In the next chapter I will look at the changes in the American Roma traditional marriage contract partly as a result of many problems with arranged marriages, in particular the *daro* or marriage payment from the groom's family to the bride's family for their loss of fortune-telling income. I will also discuss fortune-telling and ideas of luck. All of these topics are intertwined with the traditional American Roma marriage practices.

1. How does the idea of corporate identity conflict with individual identity in Roma/American context? Even though S.N. had not committed theft, why was he convicted anyway?

2. Explain the prejudices of the prosecutor and police "expert" in the Nicholas case.

3. What was the author able to do to make prison life less "*marime*" for S.N. and allow him to eat?

4. Name two reasons why the girl who joined the job corps would need to be reinstated into the Roma, and explain how this was done.

References

Clifford, J. (1988). *The Predicament of Culture.* Cambridge, MA: Harvard University Press.

Getsay, T. (1982). "GYP-sies, the People and Their Criminal Propensity." *Kansas State Fraternal Order of Police Journal* Parts I, II and III.

Kamm, H. (1993a, November 17). "End of Communism Worsens Anti-Gypsy Racism." *New York Times.* Retrieved from http://www.nytimes.com/1993/11/17/world/end-of-communism-worsens-anti-gypsy-racism.html?pagewanted=all.

Kamm, H. (1993b, November 28). "In Slovak Gypsy Ghetto, Hovels and Plea for Jobs." *New York Times.*

Miller, B. (2010). *The Church of Cheese.* Boston, MA: Gemma Media.

Sutherland, A. (1986 [1975]). *Gypsies: The Hidden Americans.* Long Grove, IL: Waveland Press. (Originally published, New York: Free Press.)

United States v. Nicholas, 900 F.2d 1264 (9th cir. 1991).

Chapter 6

Marriage, Fortune-Telling, and Luck

Marriage

The ideal marriage of the Roma is to marry a second cousin from the same *vitsa* because then the coparents-in-law *(Xanamik)* will be aunt or uncle to nephew or niece or first cousins. My friend Wally Davis, for example, is married to his second cousin, Vina. Another desirable marriage is between more distant cousins within a *vitsa* or between two closely related *vitsi.*

There are a few prohibited marriages:

- First-cousin marriage—because the *Xanamik* will be brothers or sisters, and that would be destructive to those sibling relationships, which are very important to the *vitsa.*

- Marriages that are viewed as incestuous—including any sexual relations between any man in the groom's *vitsa* (includes father-in-law, brother-in-law, and brother of groom) and the bride *(bori).*

- Marriage to a non-*Roma* or *gadjo/gadji.* Sexual relations or marriage to any of those categories is considered to be *marime* or ritually polluting and could result in the persons being outcast from the Roma communities.

Marriage is always the key point in the developmental or life cycle of the individual (from birth, baptism, childhood, puberty, adult [marriage] to death) in which Roma identity is solidified (by a successful marriage that produces children) or lost (by dissolution or marriage to a non-Roma). The groom's uncles and elder men (including his father who may not actually discuss the arrangements), meet with the important men in the bride's family and ask for her marriage to their young man. They bring a gift of a bottle of Crown Royale whisky decorated with a red ribbon and gold coins. The men discuss the virginity and purity of the bride, her beauty, and her abilities as a fortune-teller and then settle on a marriage payment from the groom's family to the bride's family. After the agreement is made, the bride and groom may be allowed to meet in the presence of their families. In the past, but no longer today, sometimes they met for the first time at the wedding.

The wedding is an elaborate celebration with a feast table where the men of the two families sit and eat together. The bride and groom act shy and do not have contact with each other, sending only quick glances one to the other. The bride may cry appropriately in sadness about leaving her family. Both she and he are obeying their family's wishes although secretly they may be very happy as well. All the other guests are happy and drink and shout out in celebration at the success of marriage. At one moment the bridal veil is put on the bride's head, and she is taken to the middle of the room to dance, led by the young men in the groom's family in a long line with a red flag at the head of the line, symbolizing that the *bori* is now the responsibility of the groom's family. During this dance the bride should appear to be dragged into the groom's family and she pulls back and weeps copiously. Later, during the meal, she comes to the men's table with a loaf of bread with the middle cut out, and the men put money in the bread for the couple's future life together. The older women, who are not seated at the table, may shout out their opinions from the sidelines, and they enjoy the dancing and drinking. When the ceremony is finished, the bride is taken to a house of the groom's family and they consummate the marriage. If she is truly a virgin, the bed sheet with blood on it is shown to everyone, and there is great joy that she has lived up to her promise and to the payment the groom's family gave to her family.

The couple is expected to produce children as soon as possible. They live with the groom's family, and the new *bori* is expected to serve her parents-in-law and keep her head down in modesty. Any money she earns from fortune-telling is given to her in-laws and used to support her husband and his family. Her status in the family is very low. Once she has children, her status improves and the marriage may be solidified. However, until this point, any disagreement between the *Xanamik* or fight between the two *vitsi* or between the bride and groom can result in the marriage being dissolved. This means the bride returns to her family and the groom's family tries to get their marriage payment returned. These battles over dissolution of a marriage can become nasty and violent and cause a permanent rift between the two families. The ones that result in violence can end in tragedy with someone badly hurt or killed and another person in jail. It is not uncommon for the couple to try to stay together in the face of enormous opposition from their families. They may have to disappear for a period of time until things cool down and they have had a baby. When the first baby is born, the *Xanamik* make a greater effort to accept the marriage.

Finally, many problems arise from the failed negotiations of arranged marriages. Traditionally the American Roma do not get a marriage license from the state or have a wedding in a church, although the Roma who have converted to Pentecostal Gypsy churches (where the pastor and full congregation are Roma) have a wedding in the church. Arranged marriages are important moments of identity shift for the individual and the *Xanamik* with whom a whole set of new relationships are created. The marriage payment that flows from the groom's family to the bride's is at once a statement of the status positions of the two families, the status of the bride's purity, and the beginning of new statuses for all concerned. There is a lot at stake for all parties involved in the marriage contract but most of all for the *Xanamik*. When the marriage fails, usually because the two families disagree rather than because the couple are unhappy, the *Xanamik* launch a status cockfight. Today, in these battles, more and more the *Xanamik* have turned to the American legal system to punish the other family. In one case, which occurred in Pennsylvania, the bride accused the groom's mother and sister of holding her down during a rape by the groom. The groom, his mother and sister were arrested, and the groom agreed to a guilty plea in return for the charges against his mother and sister being dropped. He served two years in prison for the rape of the bride his and her parents arranged in the first place. This prior conviction of "violent behavior" later contributed to his receiving the death penalty in a capital case. He has been on death row in solitary confinement for many years. The defense attorneys in his appeal, when they understood the circumstances of the rape conviction, concluded that they could not challenge it in the appeal of the death penalty because it was too unbelievable, and anyway, under American law, an individual is solely responsible for his behavior, and if he pled guilty, then he must be guilty.

Today some marriages are still arranged by the *Xanamik,* but more and more young people want to have a say in who they marry, and so their preferences are considered in the arrangement. According to Wally Davis (personal communication), his children's generation is much more involved in choosing their spouses, and if they don't get their way they may elope or get married anyway. Those who attend the Roma evangelical churches have an opportunity to meet other young people from several *vitsi* and have a much wider selection than in previous times. In addition, religion is a factor because they want to marry other evangelical Roma, and the Roma preacher is happy to perform the wedding and bypass the couple's elders.

Fortune-Telling

When I was in the thick of fieldwork, I went for a short visit to see my large and gregarious family in Texas. I was deeply shocked to find I could read their minds—could know what they were thinking in spite of what they were saying. Of course these were family members I had known all my life, and while I might naturally have insight into their mind-sets, this was something different. It was knowledge of the most private thoughts that were not spoken. Of course I did not believe I was really "reading their minds," the way I had observed some Roma women do. But I thought maybe I picked up something of their skill and knowledge. So I decided to test it. While one sister was talking, I blurted out, "but what you are thinking is . . . ," and her reaction confirmed it. I kept this up for days, and my family was becoming very suspicious, grilling me about how I could know this and that. And I was frightened by some of the thoughts that I sensed in them.

When I went back to the Roma I spent more time trying to figure out how I learned that skill from the Roma women, how they taught it to their daughters and daughters-in-law. I have never really figured it out, but I know that it starts with keen observation of every aspect of a person's body, clothing, demeanor, and speech habits and then includes putting that information together to come up with a certain amount of insightful guessing. The result is an "uncanny mind reading." It takes knowledge of the cultural practices and habits of the "client" combined with intense concentration on even the smallest detail. And of course practice: The more a woman does it, the better she gets.

I had a friend who went to a fortune-teller to have her palm read. The fortune-teller told her, "You work at Neiman Marcus [a high-end store]." My friend was totally amazed, as this was true, and she went on to believe the rest of the palm reading. I knew that my friend did not work with the public out in the store but was an accountant in the offices of Neiman Marcus. So later I asked the *romni* fortune-teller how she could have known where my friend worked. "Oh, that was easy, Annie, she was wearing clothes from Neiman Marcus and looked like she could not afford them so I figured she must work there and get them on a discount."

HOUSE OF PRAYERS
This House has an Altar for Everyone

Open 7 A.M.
Till 10 P.M.

GOD

SENT

Open 7 Days
A Week

GOD'S
MESSEN-
GER

REV. MOTHER POCAHONTAS
Spiritual Healer and Advisor
Come See Her in Person
GOD SENT. ALL PRAYERS AND HEALING TO YOU

Touch of her hand will heal you. MOTHER POCAHONTAS has the **God-Given Power to Heal by Prayer.** Everyone welcome, white or colored, at REV. MOTHER POCAHONTAS   Home. What you see with your eyes, your **heart** will believe. Are you suffering? Do you need help? Do you have bad **luck?** Bring your problems to MOTHER POCAHONTAS now and be rid of them tomorrow. She advises on all affairs of life. There is no problem too **great** she can't solve (how to hold your job when you have failed, and how **to succeed, calls** your friends and enemies by name without asking you a **single word,** and reunites the separated). Upon reaching womanhood she **realized she** had the God-Given Power to help humanity.   REV. MOTHER POCAHONTAShas devoted a lifetime to this work. From the four corners the world they have come to her, White and Colored — men and women of all races and walks of life. Guaranteed to remove evil influence and bad luck. There is no pity for those knowing they are in hard luck and need help and do not come for it — one visit will convince you. She gives lucky **days.**   Lifts you out of sorrow and darkness and starts you on the way to success and happiness. If you suffer from alcoholism and cannot find a cure, don't fail to see this Gifted Woman who will help you. REV. MOTHER POCAHONTAS is here for the first time.   REV. MOTHER POCAHONTASinvites you to her home.

REV. MOTHER POCAHONTAS   **guarantees to restore your lost Nature.**
HALF PRICE WITH THIS AD. BY APPOINTMENT ONLY.

Come and be Blessed and Healed by the   Saints. Private Counsel-ing on E.S.P. (Extra Sensory Perception) and Your Super-Conscious.

REV. MOTHER POCAHONTAS
829 PROBANDT,   SAN ANTONIO, TEXAS
PHONE 226-1122
Across the street from
Alamo White Trucking Service

Fortune-Telling flyer.

One of the questions I am asked most often about Romanies is: Do they have psychic powers? The answer is yes and no. No, because for them fortune-telling is primarily a way to make money. They do not believe they can see the future or that their cures or actions are effective unless the client believes in the cures (placebo effect). That said, yes, they believe that they do give good advice sometimes and that a love potion can work because it indicates to the recipient that someone loves them. They do think that wishing someone harm and actually putting a hex on them certainly may bring the person bad luck or be harmful. They genuinely believe in the power of good luck and bad luck. They themselves are always seeking good luck and trying to avoid bad luck for which they have a specific word, *prikaza*.

The Los Angeles market for psychics and fortune-tellers is extremely lucrative. Both Roma and non-Roma practice perfectly legal businesses for this market. Both the rich and the poor in the United States, and even some of my academic colleagues, visit fortune-tellers on a regular basis to see what is coming in their lives. It is a legitimate business when a fee is charged for "reading" the palm or tarot cards and then giving advice and predictions, or, as in Newport Beach, when a budding Roma artist draws a picture of the client's soul and interprets it for the person.

However, it is fraud when the client is deceived into parting with large amounts of money on false pretenses. The *bujo* is the classic fraud in the past and even today. A *bujo* is when a fortune-teller tells a client that his or her money is cursed and offers to lift the curse if the client will bring in the money wrapped in a special cloth which is provided by the fortune-teller. When the client brings the money to the fortune-teller, she conducts a ritual over the money and tells the client to take it home and not touch it for a certain number days. When the client opens the package she finds only cut up newspapers. A switch has been made. Today, these frauds are more sophisticated. Recently a *romni* from the Marks family in Florida was tried for defrauding a wealthy writer of romance fiction of millions of dollars while acting as the writer's personal assistant.

Still, some fortune-tellers are very good at "reading" a person and can tell the client a lot of truths about him or her just as doctors can look at a person's skin and eyes and determine that the person is ill. With carefully honed observational abilities and intelligent guessing fortune-tellers can seem uncanny in their accuracy.

Young women today who become Christians in the Romani evangelical church have rejected fortune-telling as an occupation just as they have often rejected arranged marriages. In the church's teachings fortune-telling is one of the "black arts" and therefore is associated with evil and the devil. Ironically, many Roma women feel liberated by the church from having to accept an arranged marriage or being pressured into committing fraud in fortune-telling in order to make good money. Their parents and in-laws are often angered by this change of attitude and by having to give up the expectation that the *bori* will become a fortune-teller and support their son and his family.

Luck and Mystical Ideas

What has not changed is the belief in luck. The Roma believe that a person's economic and physical well-being is determined by luck. There are three kinds of luck.

First, there is good luck, which, for those who are nonevangelicals, is derived from God and saints. Every non-Christian household has a shrine to good luck figures, including saints, Buddha, good luck plants, among others. (For the evangelicals all luck comes from God and Jesus, not from saints.) Staley and his wife, Persa, told me of a picture of St. Mary that a priest gave them when they were traveling through the United States and before they set-

Staley and Persa Costello.

tled in Richmond. With tears in his eyes Staley said, "We were very poor then. It was a hard life, but since we got this picture of St. Mary we have had luck," and Persa chimed in with, "yes and now we have our whole family here, our sons and daughters and their children and we live well now" (personal communication). They attributed their good luck to finding the picture of St. Mary in a church.

Every year, the Roma gave a feast to honor a particular saint to ensure good luck for the *kumpania*. In Richmond they gave a feast to honor St. Mary, the mother of Christ, and St. Anne, the mother of Mary. They barbeque whole suckling pigs that they have purchased on the hoof at an auction, and then the pig is butchered by men who followed ritual cleanliness practices before the butchering. They make special food *(sarme)*, such as rolled cabbage leaves cooked with rice and meat inside and then simmered in pots of melted lard. The process of cooking *sarme* is an all-day project undertaken by the women. The saint is surely pleased to have this attention and will bring good health and good luck for the family.

The second type of luck is "the luck of the *gadje*," which is bad luck. This refers to everyday misfortunes such as a flat tire or a minor accident on the road. It also includes bad luck from too close an association with non-Roma or living in non-Roma houses. Roma claim they are sick more frequently since they started living in houses, and when they do occupy a house formerly occupied by non-Roma, they first clean it thoroughly and rid it of bad spirits through fumigating it with incense. They fear too close contact in crowds of non-Roma in movie theaters, at Disneyland, and at other crowded events and spaces. Here they fear they will catch flus and colds, measles, chicken pox, and other illnesses of the non-Roma.

The third kind of luck, the kind of bad luck that brings major illnesses, such as heart disease, cancer, and diabetes, is of another dimension altogether and is called *prikaza*. *Prikaza* comes from the devil, malevolent spirits, the souls of the dead *(mulo)* who have a grudge against someone, or curses by an old *romni* who has been insulted or harmed by someone. All bad luck is a punishment for transgressions, a person's bad behavior toward others. The devil is responsible for calamities and diseases specific to the devil such as convulsions, cerebral palsy, and other diseases of the mind. A female spirit called *Mamioro* (Little Grandmother) is also malevolent. She travels by night and enters the homes of Roma. If she finds that they are not following purity practices, she is so disgusted that she vomits near the house. Her vomit *(johai)* is very valuable as it counters the bad luck and illnesses she brings.

In the same way the devil when he enters someone's body and causes convulsions he defecates, and this is also a valuable counter to the illnesses he causes. There is also a death spirit who enters the window of a room in which someone is very sick and dying. He sits on the window sill and tries to coax the sick person to follow him to the "other side." For this reason, old women who have great knowledge of incantations and medicines such as *johai* and devil's dung keep these medicines in a bag in their skirts to protect their family from illnesses. Devil's dung is thought to be able to drive the death spirit away. They curse the devil, shake smoking sticks at him, and as a last resort try to ritually defile the devil by exposing their lower body genitalia to him. With the death spirit, all they can do with these methods is delay death.

Belief in the "evil eye" is prevalent among the Roma and local cultures in the Balkans, Greece, and Bulgaria from which many American Roma migrated to the United States. Dark eyes and thick eyebrows that meet in the middle are signs of the evil eye to the American Roma. Children who are admired are especially susceptible to the evil eye and they can become sick. The antidote to the evil eye is to spit on your finger and touch the middle of the child's brow. Since I had thick eyebrows during my fieldwork, I learned to immediately put some spittle on a child I was admiring to neutralize the evil eye. The mothers were always grateful to me since they were embarrassed to ask me to do it.

While these Roma beliefs may sound strange, there are many people in the United States who believe in a number of mystical, nonscientific ideas such as:

- vaccines cause autism
- what goes around comes around
- bad vibes are harmful
- prayer helps people to recover from illness
- karma or luck plays a role in life

There is a multimillion-dollar market in homeopathic medicines that many believe can work even when there is little scientific evidence to support this idea. Many believe that organic food is healthier and more nutritious than nonorganic food, even though there is little nutritional difference between organic and nonorganic; that foods sourced locally are better for you than food brought from a distance; that the body is full of "toxins" and needs to be cleansed with special enemas periodically; and so on. The Roma understand these beliefs held by the *gadje* population at large and adapt their advice and fortune-telling to these beliefs.

Conclusion

Romani marriage is a crucial moment in the life cycle of an individual and the point at which he or she becomes an adult (*rom, romni* or *bori*) from an adolescent (*sha baro* and *shey bari*). Now that young American Roma are insisting on choosing their own mate and have access through the evangelical church and the Internet (particularly Facebook) to a wide range of choices, they can converse with and see a marriage prospect on their own before physically meeting the person. Particularly those in the Roma evangelical church are encouraged to make a love match and get married to another evangelical. The *bori* will no longer have to tell fortunes and be pressured by her in-laws to commit fraud. Belief in luck, good and bad, however, is also part of church teachings as they view good luck being from God and bad luck (particularly *prikaza*) from the devil.

Good health is also a form of good luck from God. This does not mean they rely on prayer to be healthy. They have a practical approach to illness and combine Western medicine with their own medicines. Western doctors can bring good luck or bad luck. Much of health and illness is also based on social factors and the behaviors of individuals.

In the next chapter, I discuss the health of American Roma, the relationship between health and luck, between illness and *prikaza*, attitudes about death, as well as how the Roma interact with medical professionals.

1. Which marriage partners are considered unacceptable and which are the ideal marriages for the Roma?
2. Is fortune-telling simply a fraud? What skills does it require to be successful?
3. The Roma attribute good or bad luck to what factors?
4. How is the idea of luck important to the Roma?
5. Do you have any nonscience-based beliefs similar to the Roma ideas of luck?

Chapter 7

Health and Illness

Although most Americans hardly know that Roma live in their cities, the medical profession is usually well aware of them. This is because Roma are generally not healthy and because they are assertive in seeking medical care. Roma have an unusual ability to maneuver within a complex medical system and to get attention from medical personnel. The Roma "style" of seeking help is often frustrating and confusing to health care professionals. Roma may request specific "famous name" physicians and demand specific treatment they have heard of even when the treatment or specific physician is inappropriate. Roma frequently request specific colored pills that they share with their relatives. They prefer older, "big" (well-known) physicians over younger ones. They often do not comply with preventive and long-term treatment. When a relative is sick, they come to the hospital in alarmingly large numbers, sometimes camping on hospital grounds, disregarding visiting rules, and generally creating chaos in the corridors of the hospital. Hospital personnel are often at a loss in knowing how to deal with Roma (Sutherland 1986 [1975]; Sutherland 1992a, 1992b).

However, Roma can be cooperative, interesting patients. They respect authority in their own families and the authority of the doctor. They are eager to learn about the best treatment for themselves and their relatives, and they have a large support network of relatives. All of these factors can assist medical professionals in providing treatment to Roma while reducing the disruption that results from a sick Roma's desire to have relatives nearby.

In this chapter I discuss Roma cultural practices in dealing with illness, medical places, and medical professionals. These cultural practices are general practices and ideas about the causes of illness and how to cure them, although not every Roma follows every single custom or rule. Families and individual members have varied practices. Some Roma are more old-fashioned than others; some are more fastidious; some, generally older ones, are more informed; and some are sicker and have more experience with physicians. The social context of Roma medical and religious knowledge of health and illness begins with Roma attitudes in general toward good luck and bad luck, and cleanliness and uncleanliness or impurity. Attitudes about these concepts relate, as well, to causes of illness, the health status of Roma, and the eventuality of death. Embedded in a desire to be healthy is the need to live up to the ideals of correct behavior.

Fortune and Health

Good fortune and good health are closely associated for Roma, as expressed in their most common greeting, *Devla baXt hai sastimos* (May God give you luck and health). Those who enjoy good health also have been blessed with good fortune; those who are ill have lost their good luck. To some extent everyone can influence their own fortunes. By their actions they either promote their own health or cause their own illness. Illness can be caused by actions that are considered immoral. Returning to a state of purity and conforming to correct social behavior are necessary to cure these conditions. For example, a young girl who exhibits rebellious behavior and runs away from the family brings *prikaza* to the whole family. If she has had sexual relations while away, she can only be "cured" by getting married.

Perhaps the most frustrating Roma belief physicians encounter is that the larger a person is, the luckier, healthier, and happier that person will be. A fat person is perceived as healthy and fortunate, and a thin person is pitied as either ill or too poor to eat, both of which indicate a lack of good luck. Wealth is also partly attributed to luck because although each family develops similar economic skills, some are more fortunate than others. Some families enjoy good health, grow to a large size, and prosper, whereas others are plagued with illness, family troubles, and economic failure. In such a situation persons must take action to change their fate. Personal cleanliness, proper social attitudes, and behaviors such as generosity and virtuousness should bring good luck. In a more general sense, traveling as opposed to living in one place is considered auspicious.

Roma recognize that a baby is vulnerable in the first weeks of life and take precautions to protect the child. A new baby is immediately swaddled tightly and handled only by his or her mother. The woman avoids certain foods, such as green vegetables and tomatoes, so that the nursing baby will not get colic. The child's navel is carefully cleaned and protected with ashes, and amulets are sewn into the baby's clothing for protection. In the first weeks at night, no member of the family is allowed to go in and out of the room where the baby is, and all windows and doors are kept shut lest a spirit of death, called "the night," enters to harm the baby. Crying and fear are prevented in a child by placing a small piece of ghost vomit *(johai)* on his or her tongue. Visitors are carefully watched lest they give the baby the evil eye. If the baby fusses or becomes ill, the giver of the evil eye must make a cross with spittle on the baby's forehead.

If, despite these precautions, a baby dies, this is bad luck for the parents. They must avoid the baby's body, which is buried in a secret place by the grandparents. Another way to avoid the bad luck of a baby's death is to leave the funeral and burial to the hospital authorities.

Cleanliness and Uncleanliness

Marime is a term used to indicate uncleanliness or impurity of a physical as well as a ritual or moral nature. To be "clean," the top half of the body from the waist up ideally must be kept separate from the bottom half of the body, which is considered unclean and is an area associated with feelings of shame. The source of uncleanness of the lower body is the genitoanal area and its emissions and secretions. Secretions from the upper half of the body are considered to be "clean" and not shameful. For example, spittle is viewed as a clean and a curative substance that may be used to clean cuts or scratches. This viewpoint conflicts with Western medical practice, which sees spittle as a source of germs and contagion. Separate soap and towels are allocated for use on the upper and on the lower part of the body, and they must not be allowed to mix. To the Roma, a failure to keep the two sections of the body separate in everyday living can result in serious illness. A large number of practical guidelines are necessary to keep the upper half of the body separate and pure. At the least, it is important to wash the hands after touching the lower body and before touching the upper body. Body separation is a general cultural ideal that comes into play more in public situations than in private ones, and it has implications for a physician wishing to examine the lower body. Most Roma women will not agree to a gynecologic examination or a Pap smear unless the necessity of the procedure is clearly explained as essential to a woman's well-being (Sutherland 1977).

Contact with Non-Roma

The most important social boundary for American Roma is that between Roma and *gadje*. Because they do not observe body separation, *gadje* are a source of uncleanliness, impurity, and disease. Public places where non-Roma predominate, such as public toilets, hospitals, buses, schools, offices, and jails, and non-Roma homes are also potential sources of disease. All these places are less "clean" than the home of a Roma or open outdoor spaces such as parks and woods. When they must be in non-Roma places, Roma generally avoid touching as many impure surfaces as possible, but, of course, prolonged occupation of a non-Roma place such as a hospital or jail means certain impurity. In this case the person tries to lessen the risk by using disposable paper cups, plates, and towels—that is, things not used by non-Roma.

Age-Related Cleanliness

Concern for a person's health begins at birth and is most active during the days or weeks of confinement, which is from nine days to six weeks. During this time period, Roma believe the birth substances cause both the mother and the baby to be impure. In the past, infant mortality for Roma has been high. This may be somewhat improved nowadays because more women give birth in hospitals; however, the crucial period of prenatal care is still often neglected because most *romni* would find a vaginal examination shameful. One of the reasons Roma have turned to hospital birth from home birth is the advantage to them of avoiding the impure birth substances from the lower body.

After the period of impurity from birth substances, the mother and the child are considered basically pure in body and action. As they grow, children can enjoy freedom from most social restraints and are not expected to understand or demonstrate "shame" in their actions. Physical contacts defiling to adults are not necessarily defiling to children, who need not take many of the precautions that adults do to ensure cleanliness in their daily lives. Children, for example, may eat food handled and prepared by non-Roma that postpuberty juveniles would reject.

At puberty, boys and girls are introduced to the idea of personal shame. Now both their bodies and their actions will be judged in terms of control of their own polluting secretions (menstrual blood, semen) and of "shameful" and polluting actions (sexual contact). The control of sexual relations and body cleanliness is modified by marriage and childbirth, but basically such controls last throughout married life until old age.

Women have a particular need to keep clean. Menstruation, for example, is surrounded by a number of rules to control the ill effects of this potentially polluting bodily function. When a girl first menstruates she is introduced to shame (for the Roma a painful emotion of disgrace and uncleanliness) and must observe the washing, dressing, cooking, eating, and behavioral rules of adult women, partly for her own protection and partly for the protection of men. Her clothes must be washed separately from those of men and children, and she cannot cook food for others during menstruation. She must show respect to men by not passing in front of them, stepping over their clothes, or allowing her skirts to touch them. At old age, after menopause and when sexual relations are assumed to have ceased, many of these regulations are relaxed. The aged are venerated and respected persons, both because they are politically powerful (political authority is vested in the aged) and because they now enjoy a "clean" status. One day I happily told a group of Roma adults that my father at 65 had just had a baby with his new wife. They leapt up and consoled me, muttering, you must be so ashamed. Old people are expected to be finished with sexual relations, and hence are given their "clean" status (Sutherland 1977).

Food and Cleanliness

Roma try to eat only food that is known to be pure and clean. Consequently, there are many regulations regarding the preparation and handling of food. There are no foods that are always prohibited, although some adult Roma fast on Fridays. Some foods, such as pepper, salt, vinegar, garlic, and onions, are considered lucky. To eat them is believed to encourage good health.

Eating together is imbued with great social significance. To share food with someone demonstrates respect, friendship, and acknowledgement of their cleanliness. Refusing to share food is a serious affront, implying a person is not pure and clean. The most serious punishment Roma as a group can impose on anyone is to refuse to eat with the person. To be prohibited commensality (eating together) is "social death." All rituals at which Roma express important unifying social values involve the sharing of food at a feast.

All food must be carefully prepared to avoid not just dirt, but any impurity. Cooking and eating utensils are always washed in a special separate basin reserved only for that purpose. In many households, a separate soap is reserved for food-related items, and even hands are washed only with that soap before handling food. Women in birth confinement and menstruating women do not handle food. Food prepared by non-Roma is avoided. This avoidance is not always possible, such as when in a hospital, but it can be aided by eating wrapped take-out foods, drinking from cartons or bottles, and using disposable eating implements. Roma may simply eat with their hands rather than use utensils that may not have been properly washed.

Causes of Illness

For Roma, illness is not just the concern of the individual, it is a problem of broader social importance for the group. In the past, serious illness always elicited deep concern from a wide circle of relatives willing to drop everything and rush to the bedside of the stricken. The gathering of Roma in the vicinity of a seriously ill person is partly socially mandated by custom (a cultural practice) but also is a genuine expression of concern for both the afflicted and his or her immediate relatives. At the time of my fieldwork, families came together from all over the country when someone was seriously ill. Today this practice is mostly among close relatives and family members and less a broad concern of the *vitsa*.

Roma make a distinction between illnesses that originate from the non-Roma (*gadje*) and illnesses that are exclusively part of their own world (Sutherland 1992a, 1992b; Sutherland 2004). The former can be cured by non-Roma doctors, but the latter can only be tackled by the *drabarni* (literally, "women who have knowledge of medicines"), that is, their own medical practitioners. A knowledge of Roma medicine is the prerogative almost exclusively of the oldest women. They are both respected and feared because of this knowledge.

Roma often do not have a scientific understanding of how the body functions. To them American physicians simply have a special knowledge of *gadje* illnesses and cures, a store of lore on medicines, and diagnostic and curing techniques. Not all physicians have the same knowledge or ability. To Roma, a "big" doctor is one who cures, and a bad doctor is one whose medicine does not work.

Hospitals are feared and avoided whenever possible. Most Roma will go to a hospital only if they are in serious danger of dying or if they view the situation as a crisis. Furthermore, a hospital is a hostile place for the Roma, full of non-Roma, unclean, and completely removed from Roma society. Too few visitors are allowed, so for the Roma, who want to be with their kin when ill, a hospital is close to a state of exile from their own society. For these reasons, many Roma suffer great pain rather than go to a hospital. If they have to be admitted, the one thing they know for certain is that they do not want to be alone—to be without their relatives.

Roma and *gadje* diseases overlap, but their causes are different. Most Roma prefer to try several different cures for any single illness to combat the different causes. A person who has convulsions, for example, may be rushed to a hospital where a physician can attend but will also be given devil's dung by relatives. Combining Western medicine with their homeopathic medications, such as ghost vomit and devil's dung, is a way of making sure everything is covered. In my original fieldwork, I interviewed several old women of high status because of their knowledge of medicines. One day they lamented that they were running out of devil's dung and needed me to drive them to a pharmacy where I could buy some. Ever the curious anthropologist, I said sure, but not without thinking they may be tricking me. We got into my Buick tank and meandered down the highway from Richmond to Oakland on the East Bay. They stopped in front of a somewhat shabby pharmacy and told me to go in and ask the pharmacist for some devil's s--t.

Sure now that I was being tricked, nevertheless I did as they instructed and with a straight face told the pharmacist:

"I need some devil's s--t. "

He replied, "How much?"

And then to my shock handed me a bag with a smelly, tar like substance, proving to me that in fieldwork, while one should always be alert to being tricked by informants, never, never act on that presumption.

The old women were thrilled. Later I consulted a professor of pharmacology, and he verified that what the pharmacist gave me is called *Ferula assafoetida,* an ancient medicine from India from the Ferula tap root and that indeed you can get it in certain pharmacies.

Health Status of Roma

Many Roma claim that they are sicker now than they used to be (Sutherland 1992, 1992b; Sutherland 2004). They believe it is because they travel less and live in houses instead of separately from non-Roma in camps. They explained that the closer contact with non-Roma is having a deleterious effect on their health. Recent work on the medical condition of Roma would indicate that their medical problems are in fact serious. In a study of 58 Roma in the Boston area, Thomas found that 73 percent had hypertension, 46 percent diabetes mellitus, 80 percent hypertriglyceridemia, 67 percent hypercholesterolemia, 39 percent occlusive vascular disease, and 20 percent chronic renal insufficiency (Thomas 1985, 1987). A combination of diet, which is extremely high in animal fat, and genetics could lead to the high cholesterol levels and hypertension. In this group 86 percent smoked cigarettes and 84 percent were obese. The life expectancy of Roma in the United States is between 48 and 55 years (Salloway 1973). These health problems have not diminished in the 45 years since this study.

To combat non-Roma diseases, the Roma logically turn to non-Roma physicians and hospitals. Although they are eager to try any cure they think might work, they are suspicious of physicians and tend to "shop around." A physician who acquires the reputation of being effective will find Roma patients flocking to his or her office. Physicians whose Roma patients die under their care will probably never see another in their practice. Surgery is feared, especially when general anesthesia is required, as Roma believe a person under anesthesia undergoes a "little death." Thus, Roma will gather around the bedside to muster support and help the patient come out of the anesthesia.

Despite their fear of hospitals, Roma are in general extremely knowledgeable of hospital procedure. They know what services are available and who the best physicians for specific problems are. They learn of famous clinics and learn the complicated hospital regulations, how to get around them, and how to get what they want. One study concluded that Roma receive better medical care than other urban minorities because they have figured out effective ways to use medical services (Salloway 1973). In the same way that they are willing to try physicians and hospitals to cure them, they will also try cures and medicines advertised by Mexican *curanderos,* "faith healers," and patented miracle cures. These are all *gadje* remedies. Nothing that might work is to be scorned. In some fortune-telling places the fortune-tellers may describe themselves as psychics and *curanderas.*

Roma diseases have no connection with non-Roma or with germs and therefore cannot be cured by non-Roma physicians. For these diseases the Roma must turn to their own knowledge and their own medical practitioners, the *drabarni.* The knowledge of spirits and medicines that old women have is a great source of power for them.

Serious Roma diseases are caused either by a spirit (that the Roma call *mulo*) or by the devil (*o Del*). Little Grandmother (*Mamioro*) is a specific spirit who has become a disease carrier and causes illness simply by visiting the homes of Roma. Fortunately, she only visits dirty houses, so by keeping a clean house, the Roma can keep her away. *Johai,* found most frequently in garbage dumps, is the most powerful and valuable cure the Roma have. It is a slimy mold with red striations. A mold scientist at the University of California, Berkeley, suggested that I bring Roma old women to have a look at a number of Petri dishes to identify which slime mold it might be. So several went with me and took a long time studying each Petri dish, concluding that *johai* was not there. When we left, they laughed at me and said, "Annie, ghost vomit cannot grow in a dish, anyone knows that!!"

Later, Rena Gropper at Hunter College who studied Roma, discovered "ghost vomit" on some wood chips in her garden in New York City. Thomas H. Delendick, a taxonomist at the Brooklyn Botanic Garden, identified it as the slime mold, *Fuligo septica*. A literature search showed that heretofore there had been no known economic or folklore uses of this slime mold (personal communication, 1983).

Several important diseases are caused by the devil. *Tosca* is a disease that the Roma translate as "'nerves." People who are nervous, fidgety, and worry excessively have *tosca*. A lot of Roma get *tosca*, especially the less aggressive and more sensitive ones who find it hard to keep up with the demanding, noisy, fast pace of Roma social life. *Khantino drab* will cure *tosca*. *Khantino drab* (translated as devil's dung) is also said to be found near the place where a person has been seized with a convulsion or epileptic seizure. It is believed that convulsions occur when a person is possessed by the devil and that usually the devil defecates during the convulsion. Locating the *Khantino drab* and giving it to the convulsed person will make the devil impure and drive him away.

Death

Roma can never be sure that they have done everything possible to promote auspiciousness, to keep pure, and in general to live up to the ideals of correct behavior; therefore, it is not surprising when someone becomes ill or suffers. For the Roma, illness and death are not only a personal crisis, they introduce a social crisis as well. Reporters, physicians, hospital staff, social workers, and police are all aware of a great happening when a Roma becomes seriously ill and dies. When they ask what is going on, they may be told, "a Roma king [queen, prince] has died." This reply is a way of satisfying reporters and providing a reasonable explanation to hospital staff and police of why the Roma are flocking into town in large numbers, camping on hospital grounds, and in general breaking rules and creating havoc. Although there are no kings and queens, only leaders of the large Roma extended family, death is a major crisis in a Roma family that must be dealt with in ritual.

When a young person dies unexpectedly, the relatives are so grief stricken that their behavior can become extremely wild. In one case, after the accidental death of a young man, the relatives were so distraught that they threatened physicians for "letting him die." The relatives scratched their face, drawing blood, beat themselves on the chest and head, wailed, and screamed. This behavior was an expression of extreme grief. Even in the case of a death that has been anticipated, however, it is culturally acceptable for relatives to moan and shout out to the deceased, scratch their face, or pull out their own hair.

Death at an old age is generally perceived as part of the natural and acceptable course of events, and the attitudes and feelings toward the death of an old person are very different from those toward early death. The main preoccupation of the relatives of an old person, as well as of the dying person, is to see that all preparations for the person's eventual demise have been arranged.

John Davis, also known as Rattlesnake Pete, had a "great" death. His funeral was the greatest spectacle; Janet Tompkins described his funeral to me:

> John Davis had a brass band playing Dixieland in the funeral cortege, a horse-drawn hearse complete with black enameled scrollwork and silver lanterns and drawn by two grey Appaloosas. His grave was a red-carpeted crypt with a chandelier inside in a grave site surrounded by full-sized statues of the Apostles. In front of the casket was a flower arbor with the words "Welcome to Heaven, John Davis," in gold letters. He also had flowers in the shape of his favorite fishing chair with a pole and line dangling into a flower-edged pool, the American flag, a clock with the time of his death, a car, an airplane, and a ship (because he liked to travel), a barrel of beer and beer mugs (he liked a drink), and a little white house (he was a property owner). The newspaper the next day ran a picture of the funeral cortege with the caption, "Death of a Roma King." (Janet Tompkins, Contra Costa County Social Service, personal written communication, July 1976)

Conclusion

Older relatives have an important role in the decision-making process of a Roma patient. They may even override the decisions of the patient and his or her parents. Roma can alternate rapidly between moods or styles of interpersonal interaction from extreme assertiveness to plaintive begging. However, the Roma have a strong desire to obtain the best medical treatment. English is a second language; therefore, as with their encounters with the legal system, they often do not know how to interpret the instructions of medical personnel, which are full of technical terms. Many Roma cannot read, but it would be a mistake to assume that they are therefore less intelligent. They are accustomed to dealing with complex bureaucracies and policies. Roma accept emergency measures more readily than they accept proscriptions to undertake changes in diet or lifestyle. They lack the biological knowledge to understand the connection between diets high in animal fats, heavy smoking, drinking, and no exercise and the health problems they cause. A Roma patient does not want to be alone and will be fearful and agitated if forced to be without family. Patients who are dying want to die with their family beside them at the moment of death.

In the next chapter I will discuss the topic of crime. When I did my fieldwork I had never heard of or found evidence in the literature on Roma of a single murder committed by the Roma in the United States. It may have happened, of course, but if so it was very rare. Today, major crimes are not rare among the Roma though they are a smaller percentage than crimes committed by other American groups. Roma have throughout history been accused of being criminals, mostly because of prejudice. In the next chapter I will look at current, actual crimes.

1. Explain the connections between the following Roma beliefs about health and illness:

    A. sources of health and illness

    B. health and cleanliness (as defined by the Roma)

    C. health and certain foods

    D. health and contact with non-Gypsies

    E. doctors and hospitals

References

Salloway, J. (1973). "Medical Care Utilization among Urban Gypsies." *Urban Anthropol* 2: 113–126.

Sutherland, A. (1977). "The Body as a Social Symbol among the Gypsies." In T*he Anthropology of the Body,* edited by J. Blacking, pp. 375–390. New York: Academic Press.

Sutherland, A. (1986). *Gypsies: The Hidden Americans.* Long Grove, IL: Waveland Press. (Originally published, New York: Free Press, 1975.)

Sutherland, A. (1992a). "Gypsies and Health Care." *Western Journal of Medicine* 157(3): 276–280.

Sutherland, A. (1992b). "Health and Illness among the Rom of California." *Journal of the Gypsy Lore Society* 2: 19–59.

Sutherland, A. (2004). "Roma of the United States and Europe." In *Encyclopedia of Medical Anthropology: Health and Illness in the World's Cultures,* edited by C. R. Ember and M. Ember, pp. 923–928. New York: Kluwer Academic/Plenum Publishers.

Thomas, J. D. (1985). "Gypsies and American Medical Care." *Ann Intern Med* 102: 842–845.

Thomas, James D., Doucette, Margaret M., Thomas, Donna C., and Stoeckle, John D. (1987). "Disease, Lifestyle and Consanguinity in 58 American Gypsies." *Lancet* 330(8555): 377–379.

Chapter 8

Crime and Punishment

Most scholars of Roma and activists working on Roma human rights avoid writing about crime because of the damaging stereotype of Roma as criminals. This erroneous stereotype is openly accepted among the population at large and is used as an excuse to discriminate against Roma, particularly in European countries. In trying to improve the ingrained prejudice against Roma, scholars quite rightly avoid giving fodder for the intolerant. A scholar once told me that it was very "brave" of me even to discuss crime among the Roma because it will only play into the preconceptions of the public. Mostly the police talk about what they call "Gypsy crime," a phrase that is prejudicial in itself, and they make it seem that all Roma are criminals and being a criminal is just simply part of the culture. It is a very racist point of view.

Most scholars of the Roma are understandably fearful that by writing about crime, there is the risk that readers will think all American Romanies are involved in criminal activity as some police publications imply. That implication is false and prejudicial. These self-proclaimed experts on Gypsy crime talk and write to police departments all over the United States. As mentioned in chapter 5, in one trial in which I testified, the prosecutor took me aside to suggest I read a publication called "GYP-sies and their Criminal Propensities." Even the split of the word Gypsies implies that "gypping" people is an ingrained part of just being a Gypsy. Imagine an article entitled "Latinos (or African Americans) and their Criminal Propensities" being recommended by a prosecutor. As with any group, there are individuals and families who engage in crime. Looking at crime over a historical period, however, can be a way to look at changes in society, as good mystery writers do, and that is what I want to achieve in this chapter.

If there has been so much erroneous, damaging stereotyping of Roma as criminals, why am I writing about legal cases of actual crimes? The recent increase in serious crimes and the problems Roma have understanding and dealing with the American legal regime (system of government, authorities, rule, control, command, administration, leadership imposed from above) or apparatus (the machinery of government) has come to my attention and is very distressing to the Roma themselves. As I discussed in the Sonny Nicholas case, even when no crime has been committed, as when using a relative's Social Security number, which the Roma regard as the property of the *vitsa*, it is a felony in American law. With the increase in serious crimes in the last decade, such as rape, murder, and fortune-telling fraud on a grand scale, more and more Roma are being incarcerated. Can the Roma get a fair trial? What assumptions about proof of guilt are invalid for the Roma?

The Roma have a long sordid history of persecution dating back to the Middle Ages in Central and Eastern Europe (where they were enslaved in the principalities of Wallachia and Moldavia) and during World War II when they were, together with Jews, targeted by Hitler for extermination. The Jews and Roma lost a larger percentage of their population in the Nazi-controlled areas than any other targeted group. This horrendous history is not over. It has been resuscitated since 1989. When I went to Prague in 2014 there was an exhibit with Roma testimonials that stated their lives were better under communism because they had guaranteed employment and housing and could not be killed with impunity. In the Czech Republic they have more free speech and can move around, but the local population also can freely discriminate against them. Because of prejudice about hiring Roma, they cannot get jobs, and they live in substandard housing segregated from others. This is true in many Eastern and Central European countries. In America, fewer people know who the Roma are so the discrimination is less severe. They tend to be *exoticized* by the public and vilified by the police, but for the most part they are left to live as they wish unless they commit a crime.

The American Judicial System

I am interested in crime and the American judicial system for a number of reasons. My concern is that it is difficult, maybe impossible, for Roma to get a fair trial in the American legal system. Cultural clashes become most prominent for the Roma when they are arrested and tried in American courts. Ordinary contact between Roma and *gadje* involves many misunderstandings, and the consequences of those misunderstandings can and do lead to discrimination and prejudice in their lives. Over centuries, Roma have developed effective strategies for dealing with prejudices (an exception being World War II concentration camps). Secrecy, dissimulation, and close bonding with their own people are some of those strategies.

In a court trial prejudices can be catastrophic. To American court officials, including defense teams, the behavior of the accused seems strange and incomprehensible. Motivation for the Roma can be far from the kinds of motivation the courts accept as normal. Actions that appear to be signs of guilt, such as running from a crime scene, are not necessarily a sign of guilt for the Roma but of fear of the *prikaza* of the *mulo*. When a defense attorney is baffled by his or her client's behavior the attorney calls on a "cultural expert" to help explain the "strange" behavior. A cultural defense is of fairly recent use in the courts but becomes crucial when the accused's behavior is deemed incomprehensible.

In the last few years I have been called as an "expert witness" for the defense in several legal cases involving Roma. Although conflicted by all the problematic ambiguities of acting as an "expert" in the extremely rare cases of murder by a *rom,* I was basically the only resource the defense attorneys could find to make sense of the accused's behavior. There are huge problems with the "cultural defense" since courts usually consider a cultural defense only for mitigating circumstances in assessing the penalty phase of a crime once the accused has been found guilty. I have acted as an "expert" witness on Roma culture in two capital murder cases that resulted in the death penalty, a manslaughter case, and other cases that are still pending. I have found that in these cases, there were irresolvable frictions between legal processes and Roma that a "culture expert" such as myself cannot resolve.

Being called as an expert witness involves a variety of circumstances. Initially I am contacted by defense attorneys to determine if their clients are Roma because they do not know if that is true and have little idea what it means. Then they ask me to explain why their clients refuse to cooperate with their own attorneys in preparation for their trials. The defense attorneys understandably claim they cannot organize an effective defense without the cooperation of their clients. The clients may even threaten to fire their attorney, and in one case, one of the accused did fire his attorney in the middle of the trial and waived his right to counsel during the penalty phase. With no mitigating circumstances presented and no counsel, he was sentenced to death. Later I had to explain why a Roma defendant also would not cooperate with the appeal to overturn the death penalty and preferred death to life in prison.

There are numerous cultural problems that affect the trial, beginning with the most simple—that the court, although it does try, has usually been unable to find translators of their first language, *Romanes,* for the trial. This is in fact very difficult. First of all there are no Roma who can act as an impartial translator since everyone's identity is linked to a family and *vitsa,* and impartiality is elusive at best. I have found no non-Roma who knows the language and is trained as a translator who would be willing to act as a translator in a trial. Since American Roma speak some English, even if illiterate and very limited, courts do not vigorously pursue the task of getting a translator. This is in spite of the fact that there are many important concepts in *Romanes* (e.g., *Xanamik, prikaza,* and *Mamioro*) that do not have an equivalent word in English and therefore are difficult for Roma to use to defend themselves.

Second, other Roma, even close relatives, refuse to be involved with the court or any court officials, or even to attend the trial. They gave me two reasons: fear of being "infected" with the bad luck of the person in jail and, in the case of murder, fear of physical or spiritual retribution by the victim's family with whom they felt more sympathy than with the *rom* who, in their minds, had committed a heinous crime. These relatives do not operate on the assumption of innocent until proven guilty and probably have little idea of what a fair trial would be. They are often very ashamed of their loved one. One time the mother of a *rom* convicted of murder came only once to see her son during his appeal of the death penalty, and she hid in back of the courtroom, hunkered down, covering her face because she felt so much shame.

A third obstacle the Roma face is that the usual psychological evaluation of mental health and/or IQ cannot produce any findings of value to the court. These tests almost always come up with vague statements of some kind of personality disorder. IQ tests were also inconsistent and valueless because they produced a very low IQ, in the range of borderline mental functioning, in even the most alert and articulate Roma. The basic problem with the usual tests is that the questions and context of the tests make little sense to the Roma individuals whose responses are also incomprehensible to the test givers. Furthermore, mental illness is very difficult to determine for the Roma. Much of their behavior might be considered sociopathic or borderline personality disorder simply because they do not socialize much with non-Roma and do not behave in ways that are considered "normal" in American society. Their cultural practices and beliefs are considered a pathology. They move and travel very frequently, prefer that their children are educated by them, and only engage with American society to make a living. They do not usually seek help from psychology professionals because they know that those professionals cannot assess what is normal Roma behavior. In short, no mental capacity or mental illness test has been accurate enough to be of value to the defense.

For a cultural defense to be effective as an argument for mitigating circumstances in the penalty phase of a capital crime, the jury, judge, and attorneys have to understand the rationale of the cultural circumstances of the Roma and find those circumstances credible. In my experience with explaining cultural assumptions and processes, both prosecutors and defense attorneys, other court officers, and juries often find the cultural circumstances of the crime too fantastic or absurd and therefore are unable to assess such mitigating circumstances.

The assumption that relatives want to help the accused is also problematic. Roma ideas about luck and particularly *prikasa* because the *rom* has been in jail, deter even close relatives from standing up for the accused. Jailers cannot understand why a Roma convict is not visited by his family, or why a *rom* will not eat any of the food in jail nor will he bathe or shave. Very often the only useful action I can take for them is to suggest appropriate food, clean razors, and a separate bar of soap and towel for each of the upper and lower body. When I inform the jailers that this is a religious belief, in my experience, they have been very cooperative.

Authorities also have great difficulty accepting that pooling income in cash at the home of the leader of a *kumpania* or *vitsa,* a classic anthropological redistribution system identified by Malinowski in the Trobriand Islands, is not evidence of a crime committed (Malinowski 1922). The police charge the *rom* with stealing because, on the one hand, the only way he could have that kind of money when he had very little income was to steal it. And if it was legitimate, why did he not put it in a bank? They then conclude that there is a money laundering scheme afoot. In one case, after years of litigation and with the help of an expert witness anthropologist and a scholar of Romani Studies, the *rom* finally won his case.

In spite of knowing all the prejudice and misinformation about Roma life, there is a risk that readers will think, as do many police, that all American Roma are involved in criminal activity. As with any group, there are individuals and families who engage in crime. My interest in this book is to understand changes in Roma society; looking at the increase in violent crime in the last 15 years gives a window into why and how life is changing for the Roma.

Rise in Crime and Violence

The Roma have a history of intrafamilial fights that may involve physicality, but it usually is stopped by older relatives who have the authority over younger family members. However, violent crime and murder have, in the past, been so rare I never encountered a case during my fieldwork, nor did I find much evidence of such in the literature on Roma. This has changed and is recognized by every *rom* and *romni* I have met recently who lament what is happening. The rise of violence in crime is not unique to American Roma and is evident all over post-1991 Europe and Scandinavia.

Martti Gronfers (2001) has noticed a rise in crime and violent acts among Swedish Roma who he has studied for over 20 years. He links the rise in crime to alcoholism and drugs, as well as to changes in the authority regime. Whereas elders and men have been highly respected in the past, this attitude has weakened in recent times. Ronald Lee (2001) attributes a rise in violence to the breakdown of the *kris* such as among the Mexican Roma *(Mesikaya)* where it led to a vendetta and the deaths of several Roma. These are important factors.

There has also been an influx of Roma from Romania, Bulgaria, and former Yugoslavian and Czechoslovakian countries since 1991, and of Roma from Mexico and Central and South America. Some of these newly immigrated Roma may not have had the practice of the *kris* in their country of origin (such as the Bosnian Roma), or because they have immigrated recently and are without elders and kin who can enforce a *kris* consensus decision, they represent a challenge to the authority of the "American *kris*."

Related to those immigration issues, American Roma are increasingly willing to bring in American law to settle their disputes when those disputes cannot be settled internally. Unfortunately, when one family reports another to the law, the fight escalates. In one 2005 case a marriage arranged between two families, the Millers and the Springheads, both new to the West Coast, failed shortly after because of disagreements between the heads of the *vitsi*. In retaliation someone burglarized the house of one of the Greek *rom* (in a family of Millers) for not returning the marriage payment when the marriage failed. The Greek *rom* fled, but returned and informed the LAPD of the burglary. The police found fingerprint evidence on a bottle of Crown Royale in the Miller house where the negotiations for the marriage took place. They arrested the Springhead man. When he was released on bail, he allegedly threw a Molotov cocktail through the window of Miller's mother-in-law, a fortune-teller with an office on Sunset Boulevard in Hollywood, and she died of her burns. When I talked with the accused in the LA County jail, he seemed astonishingly happy. I asked him why he was so jovial, after all he was in one of most notorious county jails in the country. He laughed that being there was not so bad because he had various relatives in the same place and felt protected (from the Springheads and Greek Millers). Also his sister had tried to kill herself because of the way the family she married into treats her and forced her to "lie on [about] my brother and he could get the death penalty." Who knows how the courts will figure it all out when it comes to trial.

The Yanko Case

Information on this case is based on interviews with brothers George and John Yanko, their mother Rose Yanko, brother Danny and his wife Nancy, and brother Caesar and his wife Mary, as well as from John Yanko's sworn testimony at his brother George's trial in which he was convicted and sentenced to the death penalty. I also worked with the attorney for the defense, the investigator who interviewed many family members, and the psychologist. I had access to the transcripts of their interviews with members of the Yanko family as well as to John and George while in prison. What follows are John and George's stories based on what they told the investigator for the defense.

When he was 14 years old, John Yanko's parents arranged his marriage to Teresa Cristo who was also a child. He did not find this unusual because his parents' marriage was arranged by his grandparents when his mother Rose was 15 and his father was 17. Teresa's parents agreed to the marriage arrangement and received a marriage payment for their permission. John and Teresa had their first child when he was still 15. By age 40 they had seven children, and John was in prison for a residential burglary.

In prison he presents himself as a Hispanic, though he is not. John is a Roma whose first language is Romanes. There are no other Roma in his prison, and since no one there knows what a Roma is, taking on a Hispanic identity provides him with an ethnicity in the hyperracialized prison system. Like most Roma in the United States, he can speak Spanish as well as English.

John's family, like many other Roma, first migrated to Mexico from Europe and then to the United States. His grandparents, Steve and Lainka Yanko, arrived in Mexico and crossed the border into the United States where John's father and mother were born. John was born in 1968 in Monrovia, California. While in prison, his oldest child, 19-year-old Gina, had her marriage arranged by John's brother, and his family sent the brideprice money to him in prison. While John was in prison his father died (in 2000), but he was not able to attend the funeral.

The Yanko family consists of ten children born in 14 years between 1960 and 1974. The father worked as a handyman in a carnival, repairing wheels on the rides, fixing swings and games, and greasing chains for the carnival. Carnival life meant constant moving from place to place for the family. During this time, Rose, the mother, was either pregnant or giving birth. They lived in at least 100 different places all over the country in New York, Chicago, New Orleans, Texas, Arizona, Nevada, and California. George was born in a car somewhere on the road outside Las Vegas because the carnival had shut down for the winter, and the family had to find somewhere to live. The children almost never went to school, were not in touch with any social services, and only rarely saw a doctor. The children were not vaccinated, and once they took George to the doctor because he had whooping cough. Even in the winter months when the carnival shut down, they moved to wherever their father could find work and a place to live for a few weeks. They lived in trailers, short-term house rentals, and even tents. By 1980 the family stopped traveling with the carnival.

The mother, Rose, was a very good fortune-teller. She told fortunes inside the carnival and around town. She sold flowers and handmade dolls on street corners. According to her sons George and John, people used to give her a lot of money for her advice. John was amazed by how much money people would offer, including a car and food for the family—whatever Rose said she needed. She would tell a man that she needed money, and he would sell his car and give the money to her. John said the only way to understand this would be to look at it as the same as falling in love. "When you fall in love with someone, you will give them money and presents."

The children also were put to "work" during the fortune-telling sessions. While Rose was telling the man about his problems and making promises to him, she told the children in Romanes to take his wallet and remove money, take jewelry and anything valuable. From an early age, four or five years old, John's mother or father would take him to a house and ask for water for the radiator or for the kids. While the home owner was distracted, the children would take anything they could find—food or valuables—and give them to their parents. John described it as "just like a job." Whatever the children brought home from a supermarket, they would show their parents, and it contributed to the family income. Sometimes his father would let him keep something he took from a store. If they did not bring anything, his father, who was a heavy drinker, would get mad and yell at them. If they showed him cookies and sodas from the store, his father would say, "good job."

John rarely went to school because they moved so frequently. Also he helped his dad repair cars and with other kinds of jobs such as blacktopping driveways or repairing roofs. His time in prison is the longest he has ever stayed in one place. There he has learned to read and write and has been taught fractions.

When John grew up, he and George did everything together, including drugs—marijuana, crack, cocaine—and residential burglaries. They would arrive at a house and tell the owner that they were termite inspectors for the city. One time the two brothers went around inspecting the house and pretending to spray for termites. They found a locked closet, broke the door, and took rings, watches and about $500 in cash. As they were leaving, the old lady offered them iced tea. When her live-in daughter returned from grocery shopping, she alerted the police and John was arrested (George escaped). That was his first conviction. "I am not proud of those scams," John said, "but that is what we did." When John went to prison, his brother George helped provide for John's wife, Teresa, and their ten children. Teresa and George's wife Shirley shared both a house and their income to make ends meet.

Then the worst happened. During another residential burglary, George was surprised by the owner of the house, they struggled, and George beat the owner to death with a hammer. John is baffled that his brother George could do such a thing. Quietly crying, John said, "Violence, it is just not done when talking people out of their money or repairing a car is so easy. We were not taught to do violence. It is a bad thing. I feel bad for my brother." In late 2007 George was convicted and given the death penalty.

George was a loner in a big boisterous family that was crowded into one place, constantly moving, yelling, coming and going all times of day and night. George would mumble to himself sometimes and get easily frustrated. He was at one time treated for seizures. Still John was shocked at his brother's crime. "He is not the kind of person to do that. It is not in our culture to be violent like that. I feel emptiness for both of the families—George's and the victim's family."

Many Roma are law-abiding citizens. Some are professional musicians, actors, and writers. Many run their own businesses. One brother, for example, repairs and renovates RVs and sells them. He also buys cheap houses, cleans and paints them, and then "flips" them, an activity he calls "legal stealing." When there is criminal activity, it tends to be nonviolent fraud or robbery. Armed robbery, murder, and other forms of violence have in the past been exceedingly rare. Murder is considered a heinous crime among the Roma. The Yanko family members that I met also personally expressed a very strong condemnation of violence and especially murder. They would not attend George's trial or visit him in jail.

I describe John's and George's cases because it so rare for a *rom* to detail his childhood and life as a Roma. George told the investigator for his defense team about his life growing up, most likely because he had nothing to lose and to get sympathy. He has been rejected by his family and his people because he killed someone, and now he is in prison. He hides his identity in prison so he can be protected by the Hispanic Brotherhood. Even though he was encouraged by his parents to commit petty theft, it was never acceptable to engage in violent crime or take major illegal drugs.

Global Influences: Recent Roma Immigrants

The next case is an example of some of the recent Roma immigrating into the United States in the last 25 years. In this case, I was contacted by investigators and prosecutors from the district attorney's office in Los Angeles County who were working with a US Department of Treasury IRS investigative team. For over two years this team had been pursuing an elaborate fraud perpetuated by a large *vitsa* of *Kalderasha* Roma who recently had immigrated to the United States primarily from Venezuela and Colombia, South America.

The frauds were very sophisticated in that they required extensive knowledge of US government immigration policies (such as issuance of birth certificates and passports), US banking laws and practices (issuance of credit cards and mortgage practices by banks and other lenders), knowledge of real estate practices (purchases and sales of property, practices of building contractors, and purchases of building materials), among other kinds of knowledge such as use of the Internet, email, Facebook, and YouTube to communicate internationally. This Columbian/Venezuelan *Kalderasha* group carried out complex and sophisticated fraud operating internationally between Venezuela, Puerto Rico, and the United States. The frauds involved many millions of US dollars, making these families extremely wealthy. The wealth was manifested in expensive property purchases in the Los Angeles area of Downey, where they would tear down the existing homes and build elaborate structures to suit their lifestyle and taste.

When I was contacted, the investigation was already advanced to the point of securing several convictions of leaders of the *vitsa* and extensive knowledge of how they operated. It was also global in reach. This was a new phenomenon for American Roma and a level of fraud far beyond the reach of most local American Roma.

History of the Group

From school and birth records of many in this group, it was clear that they had spent between 20 and 30 years living in Venezuela. How and why they originally migrated to Venezuela is not clear. They speak a form *Kalderasha Romanes*, called the New *Vlax* dialect, but their appearance is entirely that of wealthy upper-middle-class Venezuelans. Film of one of the weddings that took place in Los Angles showed young girls in sexy designer gowns and the kind of Gucci high fashion popular in South American capitals. There were other lavish displays of wealth such as diamonds and gold and expensive cars.

The Identity Frauds

For whatever reason, this group of *Kalderasha* decided to immigrate to the United States, and to do this they had to figure out a way to become legal immigrants. Several leaders of the group first came to the US in 1972. At that time their children were just a few years old. To enter the United States legally, they established contact with an employee in the Registry of Births in Puerto Rico who was paid to locate birth certificates of real Puerto Ricans of similar age to each person in the Venezuelan *Kalderasha* group. They fraudulently obtained copies of those birth certificates and used them to apply for Social Security cards in the names on the birth certificates. Sometimes more than one name and birth date for the prominent leaders of the group were obtained so they could have many identities. They then applied for passports with the Social Security numbers and birth certificates attached to applications, using their own photos for every one of the names of a real person in Puerto Rico.

The adults, now, legal citizens and residents of the United States, took out multiple credit cards with the new identities. With multiple credit cards they could make purchases until the card was invalidated due to lack of payment. In the 1990s they began purchasing real estate. During the heyday of lending and easy money that led to the collapse of mortgages and the housing market in the United States in 2009 this was easy. They applied for the loans with falsified letters claiming they held a position in real or fake companies. With the loans they bought cheap houses and either fixed them up a bit and flipped them or tore them down and built new houses cheaply. They sometimes stole construction materials from other building sites to reduce the cost of building the homes or paid for materials with credit cards until they were cancelled.

In some areas of Los Angeles, such as Santa Ana and Downey, they bought up as many houses as possible in entire blocks, tore down the houses, and built fabulous homes for themselves that were interconnected to each other. There were so many purchases in Downey, the mortgage investigators dubbed them "the Downey group."

The Theft Schemes

With personal information based on the true identities of real persons, they took out multiple credit cards to make purchases of luxury goods. They applied for loans from credit agencies and filed tax forms in order to get tax refunds. The income tax returns report false income earned, names of dependents, and claim Earned Income Tax Credits in the names of citizens of Puerto Rico who had never filed income taxes. Even some of the federal administration's stimulus funds were obtained.

They used multiple addresses that they could control, mainly commercial mail drops and mail box services that they opened with the false identities in order to receive documents and checks that could not be traced to any residential address or person. When they were arrested, as many as 50 uncashed US Treasury checks were found in their homes.

The two elder leaders of the *vitsa* and other family members took the names of many living Puerto Ricans. In order to keep track of who was using which identity, the leaders kept the records of original and copies of Puerto Rico birth certificates, Social Security cards, and a photo album with pictures of real members of the group next to the aliases they were using.

They also had many mail box keys at their home addresses for mail boxes in Los Angeles and other cities in California. A suitcase in their storage unit held keys for 37 mail boxes in the Chicago and greater Chicago area. The mail boxes were rented using a false Washington state driver's license with a picture of the *rom* who was falsely using the name Miguel Valedon.

Angel Melendez, for example, is actually a poor man who is a resident of a small town in Puerto Rico who had never traveled to the United States or taken out credit cards in his name. The Venezuelan *rom* who took his name applied for credit cards and loans of hundreds of thousands of dollars as Angel Melendez. Even when he was convicted of identity theft and fraud in obtaining loans, he was convicted under the name Angel Melendez. His Roma name was never known by the court, but under the name of Angel Melendez he served 33 months in Lompoc Prison and had to pay restitution of $418,000 to the lending company.

One of the biggest frauds took place between 2008 and 2009. A *romni* taking the name Angelica Rivera contacted a woman employee in the credit industry, who was one of Rivera's tenants, and introduced her to Henry Paul Mejia. Mejia is a prominent *Krisnitori* for the Venezuelan Roma and a leader. Angelica and her husband Charlie Hernandez, along with Mejia, met with the employee to get her help for approval of a $50,000 line of credit for Mejia. Mejia told the employee that he had paid someone for this personal identity information and therefore it was legitimate information of a real person. Mejia, convinced that the employee was friendly to the operation, showed her his laptop with 5,700 Social Security numbers and tax returns. It was later found that he had obtained the identity information by breaking into schools and hospitals and stealing the records or buying IDs from poor people or homeless people. The employee checked some of the Social Security numbers to confirm that they were indeed valid IDs.

Mejia wanted to open 100 different lines of credit with the IDs and offered to pay the employee 10 percent of any credit they obtained, but the employee had already contacted US government agents who were audio- and videotaping these conversations. When they raided Mejia's home, they confiscated the computer and found scanned original Puerto Rican birth certificates, Social Security cards, copies of tax returns that had been filed with the IRS, and files containing at least 20,000 Social Security numbers and other identifying information. Mejia pled guilty to wire fraud and identity theft with the purpose of committing felonies. In January 2010 he was sentenced to 30 months in prison.

Angelica Rivera, who participated in the scheme with Mejia, had at the time already received in 2006 a loan of $663,400 to purchase a house in Corona, California, by claiming she was a sales manager for a property company and earning $16,555 per month. In 2008 she took out a second loan on the property for $165,600. After she was arrested in the fraud with Mejia in 2010, she was sentenced to serve 45 months in prison and pay restitution of $395,500 to the victim. Her husband, the son of one of the leaders, was using the ID of Charlie Hernandez, also a real person living in Puerto Rico. He was also was convicted of aggravated identity theft and imprisoned for 24 months

Part of the scheme was to file false tax returns and obtain US Treasury tax refunds in the names of real people who did not know this was happening. Another of this group, using ten different names, obtained 17 US Treasury checks that had been mailed to a UPS store in Sparks, Nevada. Law enforcement authorities also found in his home 37 US Treasury checks payable to 27 different people based on fraudulent tax returns filed with the IRS as well as checks for federal stimulus money for a total of $82,786. All of these Venezuelan Roma were convicted and jailed as John or Jane Doe without the court knowing the real names, dates of birth, or countries of birth of any of them.

Eventually, some in the Venezuelan group married American Roma and taught them how to commit the frauds. Another American *rom* father and his 20-year-old son (likely married to one of the Venezuelan *Kalderasha* girls) of the American Davis *Kalderasha* family both pled guilty in the first months of 2010 to obtaining loans for two separate houses in Corona, California, through false identification. As yet, the future impact of such sophisticated crimes being spread to American Romanies cannot be determined.

I asked Wally Davis, whom I had befriended (see chapter 6), if he had heard of the Venezuelan Roma. Yes, he had, but the American Roma call them "the Colombians." He knew they perpetrated very sophisticated crimes that he had never heard of and that American Roma had never done. He seemed both impressed with them and scared of them. Then I asked him about the Bosnian Roma who came over after the breakup of Yugoslavia in the 1990s. Yes, of course, he knew about them and he was astonished, "They have jobs," he exclaimed with incredulity. The Bosnian Roma were refugees whom I met in Minnesota. The men and women worked in a turkey processing factory. I visited the factory where the women and men wore white overalls and hats and worked the assembly line of turkeys being killed, gutted, and plucked and at the end wrapped whole or cut into pieces. It was grueling, smelly, and poorly paid work. But they were willing to take the jobs that most Americans would not. Their low-rent homes were clean and heated. For the *slava*, they killed lambs in their garages where the blood froze on the ground, but both neighbors and police were not happy about this practice.

Romanian Romanies also have fled to the United States as well as all over Europe from the dire poverty and repressiveness of Romanian governmentality as well as neighbors and the general public. Their condition is one of the worst in Europe. Only the very lucky make it to asylum in other countries.

This influx of different groups with very different *Romanes* dialects and other languages and customs is having an influence on American Roma who for the first time are living near 21st century migrants from South American and Europe. The globalization processes that have caused migration of millions of people throughout the world have also led to new immigrations of Roma. They are now exposed to cultural practices that have evolved in very different environments. The breakup of the Soviet Union, Yugoslavia, and Czechoslovakia, and the consequent freedom to travel for the first time in 50 years led the Roma to go on the move again. Then membership in the European Union created seamless borders so that they only needed an EU card to go to Western Europe, Great Britain, and Scandinavia, richer countries with social benefits that brought them out of poverty. Some Western European countries have tried to deport them back to their own countries with very little success. The fierce prejudices and persecution in their own countries have now infected the West where also, according to many Europeans I talked with, "no one likes the Gypsies."

In addition, in America where surveillance and identity markers are computerized, they cannot escape the notice of the authorities anymore and are being incarcerated more frequently. On the other hand, contact with other groups and with relatives via email, Facebook, the "Gypsy hotline" (in Los Angeles), and Twitter is connecting these very fragmented groups to each other in a way never experienced before.

Many of the Roma have converted from the old orthodox religious practices to newer evangelical protestant practices. Those who do convert now congregate in "Gypsy churches" in each city crossing the boundaries of the older *kumpania* formations. The women challenge the authority of fathers and fathers- and mothers-in-law to control their lives. As one evangelical *romni* said, "I follow Jesus Christ and God is my father. My father-in-law is furious, but I am not scared of him anymore and tell him that obeying God is more important than obeying him." The young people want to choose their own spouses although many marriages are still arranged. Homosexuality, which in the past was considered heinous, is becoming more acceptable. Wally mentioned two female *romni* who live together and are still accepted by the *vitsa*, something that would have been *marime* in the past. The evangelical preachers have become respected leaders even though they are much younger than the *rom baro* leaders. Wally told me he was very proud that one of his daughters is married to a preacher. In the same breath he lamented the loss of the "old ways" and the rising use of drugs accompanied by previously unthinkable violent acts and murders.

1. In what ways are the post-1990 Roma immigrants different from the American Roma who came in the late 19th century?
2. Why do Gypsies have an American name and a Romani name? Is the American name the same as an alias?

3. What role does 21st century surveillance play in making the traditional strategies of Roma who commit crimes no longer effective?

4. When a marriage arrangement fails, how does it lead to violent crime?

5. What is a cultural defense? When is it used?

References

Gronfers, M. (2001). "Institutional Non-Marriage in the Finnish Roma Community and Its Relationship to Rom Traditional Law." In *Gypsy Law: Romani Legal Traditions and Culture*, edited by W. O. Weyrauch, pp. 149–169. Berkeley: University of California Press.

Lee, R. (2001). "The Rom-Vlach Gypsies and the Kris-Romani." In *Gypsy Law: Romani Legal Traditions and Culture*, edited by W. O. Weyrauch, pp. 188–230. Berkeley: University of California Press.

Malinowski, B. (1922). *Argonauts of the Western Pacific*. London & New York: Routledge Classics. (Reissued, enhanced edition, Long Grove, IL: Waveland Press, 2013.)

Chapter 9

Changing American Roma Culture

Religion and Fortune-Telling

The conversion to evangelical Christianity, with an exclusive Gypsy congregation, has been taking place in California since the late 1970s and early 1980s and has brought numerous changes to the American Roma. The *Kalderasha* are converting rapidly to evangelical and Pentecostal Christianity. Although there are some *Machwaya* evangelical churches, most have continued to practice Orthodox Christianity, the traditional religion in places they migrated from (in the Balkans, Greece, and Russia).

Tom Merino is particularly disillusioned with the *Machwaya*. Yet Tom does not like the Assembly of God and other Pentecostals who are mostly *Kalderasha*. In Slovakia, he told me, Pentecostal church missionaries came and created Pentecostal Gypsy congregations. To Tom, this was like "spiritual and emotional rape," when what the Slovak Roma wanted was human rights. In the US, the pastors all compete with each other and tell their congregations not to go to other Gypsy churches. The pastor, not the *rom baro* of a *kumpania*, has become the leading authority, and pastors are competing for Gypsies to come to their churches.

Tom resisted the church at first, but "along came Jesus in the 1970s." Larry, his brother-in-law, told Tom he could not be seen reading the Bible. But Larry studied at a Lutheran seminary and became a Lutheran pastor.

In 1975 Larry Merino, a *Machwaya*, married Tom Merino's sister, Sonia, also a *Machwaya*. In 1980 Larry and Sonia became Christians and soon converted to an evangelical branch of the Lutheran religion; they decided she

97

would no longer tell fortunes, which the Bible says is a "black" art connected to the devil. Larry's grandfather, the leader of the family, found their decision unacceptable: *Machwaya* women, who have to support their husbands and in-laws, are good at fortune-telling and make enough money to support the husband's family. The men help set up the fortune-telling business, but according to Tom Merino, the men then drive around in their cars, as well as spend time playing golf. He also argued that to make good money from fortune-telling you have to "prey" on people's weaknesses, whether it be love lost or illness.

Sonia told her father-in-law she would not tell fortunes any more. Jesus is her lord. Her in-laws protested but her father-in-law finally said, "I cannot fight God." But the grandfather told everyone to blackball (*marime*) the couple. For a number of years they did, but now Larry is invited to funerals and has some contact with his family. Larry Merino has written a book about his life as a *Machwaya* and later as a convert to Lutheranism (Merino 2014).

The *Machwaya* for the most part have not become evangelicals, primarily because it would require women to stop telling fortunes and the men would have to work. They feel themselves to be superior to the *Kalderasha* and *Kuneshti* as many have told me, because those Roma do not follow as strictly as the *Machwaya* the rules regarding *marime*. Also, Larry Marino once brought an evangelical preacher to the San Francisco *Machwaya* to get them to convert to the religion. The *Machwaya* completely rejected the religion, mainly because they want their women to tell fortunes and continue to support the men. They still keep the Balkan practices of *slava* on Saint's Days and *pomani* for funerals put on by the *vitsa*.

According to Larry Merino, when he grew up he was told that if you stick with the Gypsies, they will take care of you, but that is not happening any more. Larry says many *Machwaya* are depressed and unhappy, very disillusioned. Because fortune-telling is the primary way the women make a living, the men are fighting over lucrative territories. The Newport Beach fight over fortune-telling places has ended up with physical fights, cursing each other's ancestors, reporting each other to the police, and filing law suits against each other. The Millers and the Marks families fought so much over control of lucrative territories, one girl killed herself rather than tell fortunes in such an atmosphere.

Technology and Traditions

The *kris* still functions with the *Machwaya* and some *Kalderasha*, but instead of gathering in one place to hash out the issues, they use speaker phones and Skype to communicate between San Francisco and Los Angeles. They keep in contact now using Facebook and YouTube. They still make people *marime,* but it is a much weaker punishment because people are choosing whether to obey or not, so the blackballed person will have plenty of relatives and friends who ignore the *marime* decision. As Wally Davis dramatically put it to me, "*Marime.* So what. People ignore it."

Young *Machwaya* and *Kalderasha* use technology with ease. Through videos on YouTube they can see other Roma they have never met. Then they can contact that person on Facebook, and may find someone they want to marry. They are also practicing more sexual freedom. They get married by eloping. These Roma elopements may last weeks, not years. One *Machwanka* has a 22-year-old daughter who is on her third marriage—each one an elopement. Fatima, the niece of one *Machwaya* man, was not raised to learn to tell fortunes, so her in-laws want her to do the "sweetheart scam"; that is, go to the mall and find an older man who has money and court him, flirt with him, but not have sex with him by claiming to have fortune-telling powers that would be ruined if she had sex. Even if Fatima's scam works, she eventually has to marry a *Machwaya rom.*

Visit with Wally Davis and His Church

When Wally Davis emailed me in 2014, he asked for photos of the Roma from the Richmond *kumpania,* of which he was a part. Gripped with *nostalgia* (a sentimental longing for the past, not always accurate, but indicative of a person's values) for the "good old days," Wally begged me to organize a reunion of the Romani school in Richmond where he learned to read and write. Because of his experience with literacy, he has made sure his daughters were educated in a public school until they were age 12; then they were home-schooled so they could continue learning without their reputation being tainted by being in contact with boys after puberty. This approach is working very well for California Gypsies because there is a huge support system for homeschooled children and because it has kept girls' reputations intact.

The former teachers and I visited Wally and his second cousin and wife, Zena, in their very nice condo in Sacramento. Wally lamented that the former students either had moved from California or were deceased. He and his wife Zena prepared a big lunch for us and an even bigger dinner in our honor. Zena made several traditional dishes: a healthier version of *sarme* (rice with oil and not lard, shrimp and tomato paste, basil and parsley), a barbecued

Wally and Zena Davis.

beef slab with spices, grilled vegetables, and *pirogue* for dessert (noodles with lots of sugar, eggs, butter, and cream baked in the oven). Both *sarme* and *pirogue* are traditional Balkan Roma dishes. "We have gone healthy now, Anne," he told me. "Not like the old days, but like Americans."

We spent the day looking at hundreds of pictures of the Richmond Roma we had scanned onto a laptop. It was very emotional for Wally. He recognized every man, woman, and child in the pictures and even knew their birth dates and whether they were still alive. Most were not, even though many were younger than Wally, who just turned 50. Pinky had died in childbirth when she was only 18. Staley Costello's sons, apart from Johnny, are all deceased, including all the sisters and brothers who would have been in their 60s today if they had lived. Some had died from overdose of painkillers, but most from heart disease, due to high blood pressure and very high cholesterol combined with diabetes that was not treated consistently. Obesity was a factor, and Wally, who had managed to lose 90 pounds from eating "healthy," still could barely walk with a cane due to obesity and all the other usual afflictions, such as diabetes, high blood pressure, and cholesterol. Yet he was one of a few who has survived to the old age of 50. He is amazingly alert and has kept his phenomenal memory of all the Costello and Davis families from the *kumpania* I studied. In my lifetime in academia, I have met only a couple of people with such a sharp memory for detail, including myself.

All of Wally's relatives have become "Christian" (as opposed to Orthodox Christian) in the last 15 years with their own congregation that is almost exclusively *Kalderasha* (one *Machwaya* man has been allowed to join, as he is a good singer). Wally's church is one of the largest congregations of *Kalderasha* and is located in Fremont at the south end of the East Bay. Pastor Blazo Yanko is the head of this church, and Wally's daughter, Peaches, is married to Peter, Pastor Yanko's son.

Peaches and Peter took me to the "God's Gypsy Christian Church of Praise Ministries" founded in 1988. The outside of the church was a unit in a business park in front of which a banner was affixed for the service and then removed after the service was over. An outsider would never have known where the church is located. Because they no longer practice the *slava* and *pomana*, these Sunday Gypsy church services are the only formal gatherings of *Kalderasha* from all over the Bay area. Church has now become the time and place for Gypsies to be together.

Pastor Blazo Yanko had agreed that Wally could bring me to the church service, and he greeted me at the door to say I was welcome. His wife came forward to meet with me, and then I sat next to Peaches in the furthest back row of pews, where the wives of the churchmen, who perform the service and music at the front of the church, sat with their children (all of whom were watching videos on their smartphones). The men gathered at the front to sing, pray, and praise Jesus. There was no set time for the service to begin. People started coming around 3:00 P.M., and the congregation trickled in until about 4:00 P.M., when about 120 Roma were there listening to the singing, with accompanying drums and guitar music blasting out of speakers. The service lasted two hours—the sermon was 45 minutes. Pastor Yanko preached primarily in English with some *Romanes* phrases sprinkled into the sermon. The service was very high-tech and included PowerPoint Bible stories projected on the back wall, music mixers, and other electronic equipment. The young men monitored everything from computers at the back of the room.

The front of the church had no altar, just a raised stage where the electric guitar players and a drummer with the full set of drums and cymbals were playing behind a plastic screen. There was a simple white cross on the wall on each side of the podium. All during the service, members of the congregation stood up and walked forward to the podium, their arms raised to praise God and witness and pray. At the podium the men stood together under the right cross, arms around each other praying, and the women did same on the left, hands raised, praying in a show of true devotion. On the left side of the podium next to the other white cross the Israeli flag flew, indicating where the birth of Christianity resides. In discussions with Wally he seemed not to equate the flag with the State of Israel but with the Judaism that led to the birth of Jesus, the son of God. Abraham, he assured me, had one son with an Arab mother and that led to all Arab populations whereas the son from his wife led to Judaism and ultimately Christianity.

In the pews men and women sat together with no sex separation as had been the custom in the past. People were very dressed up, the men in suits and ties, the women in fashionable tight dresses with long skirts, six-inch heels, and large, gold costume jewelry. Peaches explained that outside of church women could wear short skirts, even shorts and nobody cared, although she had to be careful that no one from the church would see her like that because the pastor is her father-in-law.

After the service a group of us went to a local eatery, The Country Inn, a favorite with the Gypsies. Wally met me there, and there were orders of "Gypsy fries" (an enormous turkey platter of French fries, covered in melted cheese and topped with thick gravy), dinner-plate-size pancake stacks smothered in butter, roast beef two inches thick topped with thick gravy (Zena was disappointed that the roast beef did not have bread between the beef slices), and corn and rice soup thickened with cornstarch. On Sunday I assumed that eating "healthy" was disregarded.

At The Country Inn I met Pinky's son Richard, who never knew his mother because she died having him when she was 18, and other relatives of Wally all of whom were under 40. The adults all knew "Gypsy," they said, but they spoke to each other in English. Their children never spoke *Romanes* at home, although they heard it spoken. Their mothers claimed that when the children started school they would begin to speak *Romanes* because they could speak to their cousins without the other kids knowing what they were saying.

"Nostalgia"

There seem to no longer be *kumpania* and *rom baro*. Families socialize in their homes but only get together in large groups in church; there are no *pomani*. They have a church funeral service and burial. Marriage takes place in the church led by the pastor. They do not celebrate *slavi* saints days, and they no longer rely on saints for good luck. Instead they celebrate the "Christian" Christmas and Easter for the birth and death of Jesus, as well as American holidays such as Thanksgiving and the Fourth of July.

The *kris* is held only for monetary grievances and can be called by anyone, even someone as young as 18. No one becomes *marime*, or blackballed, as they call it nowadays. Young people run off together when they want to get married and these issues of purity and morality are never brought to a *kris*. Peaches, when she was 20, and Peter, when he was 17, ran off together for six hours, and when Wally discovered she was missing from her bedroom in the morning he called his other daughter. She told her dad not to worry because Peaches was with Peter. Wally then called Blazo and said his daughter ran off.

Immediately Blazo said, "That is awful, let us pray."

Wally said, "I don't want to pray; go look in your son's bedroom and see if he is there."

Blazo came back to the phone upset, but then the couple contacted their families. Peaches was kept at home until she and Peter could be married by Peter's father. They were not allowed to have a Christian wedding, however. Many marriages are still arranged, but if the young couple thinks there might be any opposition to the marriage, they simply elope and the parents quickly get them married.

What really makes Wally sad is that a sense of community they once had no longer exists. "When my brother Nick died no one came (other than Wally's daughters). The old people who have not converted to 'Christianity' are not given a funeral in the church. One old lady was in the morgue for a month before any relatives came to bury her. That was unheard of before."

Wally was filled with nostalgia, longing for the "old days when you, Annie, knew how things were." He cried,

> *When someone got very sick, they all flocked to the hospital and to the funeral. The living were never left alone day or night. Everyone brought food or took up a collection for the family so ones far away could come. People took care of each other. That is gone now. In the past anyone could drop by the house and you would feed them, they could stay the night. Now you have to phone if you want to visit, and they often say, "No. We are busy." Someone throws a party and makes a lot of food and hardly anyone shows up. The saddest thing is the loss of community. We never visit with the* Machwaya. *They keep to themselves and we keep to ourselves.*

The Machwaya *still have the* slava *and* pomani *and* kris. *They are mostly not Christian and only go to a priest for baptism of a baby. The ones who have become Christian have their own churches and we do not go to their churches, and they do not come to ours. In the past we all were part of the* kumpania, *we had* slavi *together, and we all went to the* pomani. *Now everyone keeps to his own kind. The children are not taught our language, go to school, and have no respect for elders. We don't even have any elders anymore. They are all dead.*

Conclusion

Since I studied the American Roma 45 years ago, they have changed in many fundamental ways.

- The biggest changes are because of a proliferation of new evangelical or Pentecostal Gypsy churches both in Europe and the United States, which have trained preachers and targeted the Roma population specifically. While before they were united through their beliefs and rituals, now they are divided by religion. The Orthodox and Catholic churches that were a venue for baptism and Saint's days (but not marriage) are being rejected, although many *Machwaya* still keep those traditions. Baptism, marriage, and funerals are now performed in their own Gypsy Christian church by a Gypsy preacher. Sunday service is now almost the only time *Kalderash* (or *Machwaya*) from one area gather together. Even funerals consist mainly of close family members, and the traditional idea of all Gypsies helping each other in times of need is a dying practice. The church teaches them that they cannot tell fortunes (the Bible says so) and if they steal or cheat *gadje*, they will be kicked out of the church.

- Women who have converted no longer have fortune-telling as a way to contribute to their families' income and thus have lost their economic power. They are expected to stay home and raise children in nuclear families, obey their husbands, and behave modestly. The men now have to travel hundreds of miles to other states to collect scrap metal and support their families. Some have opened small businesses such as restaurants.

- They have become literate and embraced new technologies: Facebook and email to communicate with Gypsies throughout the United States and all over the world, as well as digital cameras, with which they post pictures of their weddings and church services on YouTube.

- They lost the *kumpania* through which they carried out not just economic activities, but also shared in rituals such as the *slava* and *pomani*—gatherings with huge numbers of Gypsies. They, therefore, have become more segregated from each other associating more with Roma from their own *vitsa* (both for work and church) and less with a wider group of *vitsi*. However, they have better communication with Gypsies beyond their homes and are more aware of many Roma who are different from them.

- There is a new wave of Roma immigration into the United States since the 1990s: Bosnian Muslim Roma, Romanian *Romungro* and *Mesicaya*, Venezuelan *Kalderasha, Lovara* and other former Soviet bloc Roma bring different cultural practices, languages and dialects in *Romanes*, as well as a new sophistication and higher educational level to the American Roma.

- They speak English in the Gypsy churches—in the sermons and among each other in the congregation—in restaurants, and in other public places. Children go to American schools and parents speak English with their children. Children speak fluent American English but are not as fluent in *Romanes*.

- When I reported the changes in Gypsy language practices, many scholars assumed the result was a loss of Gypsy identity. I disagree with that assumption. I see a strong and lasting sense of identity as Roma despite rapidly changing cultural practices. After all, they survived slavery in Romania, the Holocaust of World War II, and the collapse of the Soviet Union in 1989. After 50 years of being forced to take jobs and not travel in Soviet-controlled countries, they have picked up traveling again all over Europe and to the Americas. Some individuals have become assimilated, or as they put it, "become American." Others firmly resist. I do not know what further changes may occur, but, Roma identity will survive. It has always survived.

1. Those Roma who have embraced Pentecostal Christianity have dramatically changed their lives. Discuss those changes.
2. What 21st century technologies have Roma today welcomed into their lives and why?

3. Will American education and the practice of mostly speaking English mean Roma will become assimilated to American culture? Why or why not?

4. What work are men and women now doing now that Christian converts are not allowed to use fortune-telling to make a living? Has this changed the roles of men and women and, if so, how?

Reference

Merino, L. (2014). *No Word for Love: Gypsy Sense and Nonsense*. Fort Wayne, IN: Couragio Press.